Schöningh

Discover ...

TOPICS FOR ADVANCED LEARNERS

edited by Engelbert Thaler

Globalisation
Blessing or Curse?

by Jürgen Einhoff, Klaus Hinz and Karl Heinz Wagner

Sprachliche Betreuung: Josephine Einhoff

www.schoeningh-schulbuch.de
Schöningh Verlag, Jühenplatz 1–3, 33098 Paderborn

Druck 5 4 3 / Jahr 2013 12 11
Die letzte Zahl bezeichnet das Jahr dieses Druckes.

Umschlaggestaltung: Franz-Josef Domke, Hannover, Foto: Hans-Jürgen Burkard
Druck und Bindung: westermann druck GmbH, Braunschweig

ISBN 978-3-14-040059-6

Contents

Getting started

The Road to a Globalised World

The following maps show how continents and countries have been joined in the course of centuries.

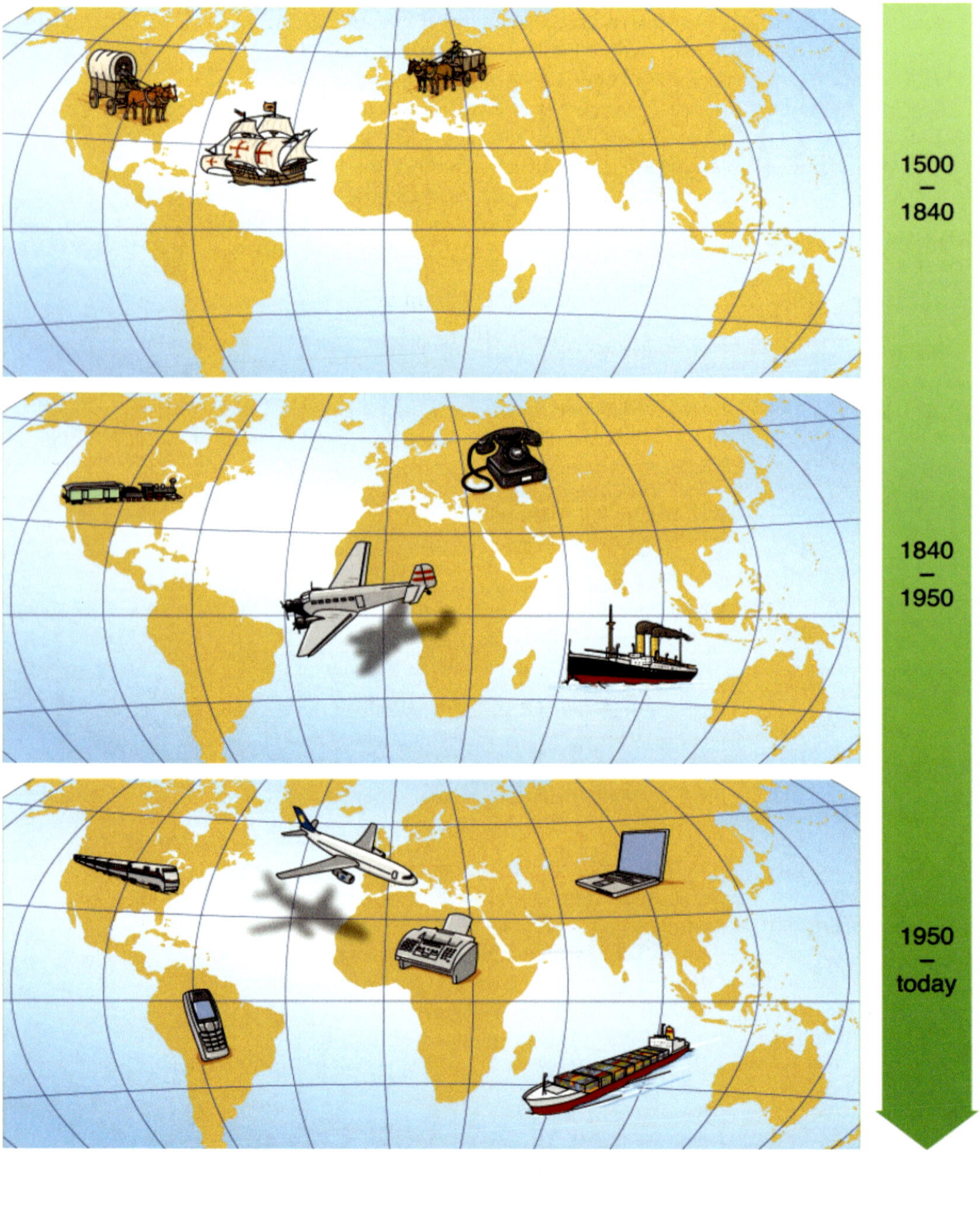

The process of linking countries and continents has led to a "globalised world", to a "global village". Marshall McLuhan coined this term in his book *The Gutenberg Galaxy*. He describes how electronic mass media cause space and time barriers in human communication to collapse, thus enabling people to interact and live on a global scale.

The process of globalisation, i. e. the connection of many different countries all around the world, has mainly been influenced by the explosive evolution of transport, communications technology and English as a world language.

In this reader, globalisation will be dealt with in three chapters. We will be looking at economic issues (trade and the management of money), socio-cultural aspects (positive and negative results of the encounter between people from different cultural backgrounds) and global challenges that politicians and institutions or organisations try to meet in order to solve global problems.

Activity

Aspects of globalisation

What points could be dealt with in each chapter? List them as follows:

economic issues	global challenges	socio-cultural aspects
....	....	....
....	....	....
....	....	....

From Country to Country – Economic Globalisation

Economic Globalisation: Past and Present

The term **globalisation**, economically speaking, refers to the increasing integration of economies especially by way of trade and financial flows. Financial markets are areas of international finance, in which large transactions are made by banks and other financial institutions. World economy is viewed as a single market.

Overview of events leading to globalisation

16th century	first great expansion of European capitalism
1870 till 1913	period of prosperity: wide expansion of world trade
Beginning of 20th century	interruption of the globalisation process
1970s	beginning of the modern globalisation period; wide expansion of capitalism; development of multinational companies The term "globalisation" was first coined in the 1980s though the concept stretches back decades or even centuries.

Today anything can be produced anywhere in the world and sold everywhere. The following are just a few of the products you can get in your home country.

Activities

Products from abroad

The collage shows a lot of things that are or may be produced abroad.

1. Choose one of them and point out the consumers' or your own benefits. Write a short paragraph.
2. What may be the disadvantages for your own country and for you as a consumer?

Coca-Cola: A Global Player

The Coca-Cola Company's headquarters are located in Atlanta, Georgia. Although Coca-Cola was first developed in the United States, it quickly became popular wherever it was sold. The first international bottling plants opened in 1906 in Canada, Cuba and Panama, soon followed by many more. Today, the company produces nearly 400 brands in over 200 countries. More than 70 percent of the income from Coca-Cola products comes from outside the U.S., but the real reason Coca-Cola is a truly global company is that all their products meet the varied taste preferences of consumers everywhere.

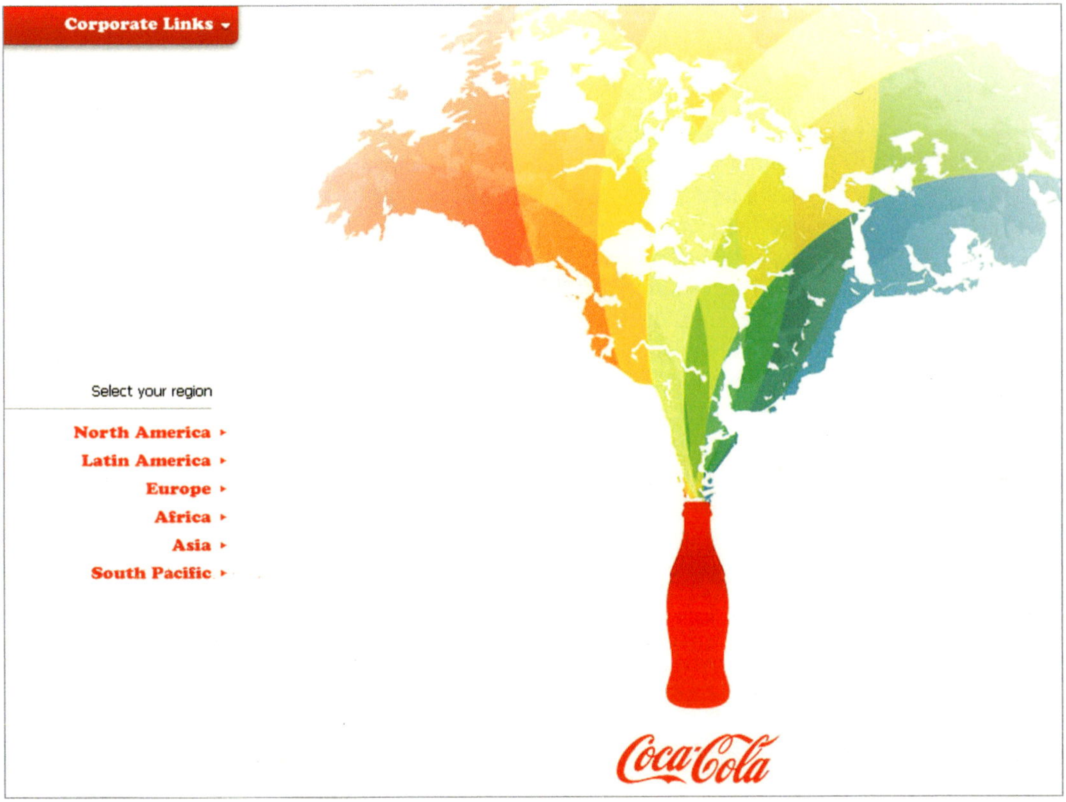

Activities

1. Together with a partner, search the Internet for more information on the history of Coca-Cola (e. g. http://en.wikipedia.org/wiki/Coca-Cola).
2. The Company sells Coca-Cola products across the globe. Take a look at some of the Coca-Cola websites (www.Coca-Cola.com) to discover where Coca-Cola beverages are sold. Select the region: North America, Latin America, Europe, Africa, Asia or South Pacific.
3. What are the advantages of big global companies on the world market?

Coca-Cola around the world

What Drives Globalisation?

Martin Wolf

The economic integration of countries is driven by two forces: a) the reduction in the costs of transportation and communications and b) economic liberalisation, e. g. the openness of markets across the borders.
The reduction in the costs of transportation and communications has not changed in the past, though it has increased in speed over the past two centuries. Economic liberalisation, however, is far from being constant: the last two centuries have seen two upswings and one huge downswing (cf. table p. 6).

While reading the ▼ article take notes on the driving forces of globalisation: a) transportation, b) communications technology.

Changes in transportation and communications technology create opportunities for increased commerce and are, in turn, created by them. This is not a new phenomenon. The railway, the steamship, the refrigerator, and the telegraph created the opportunities for the integration of the 19th and early 20th centuries. The railway made the shipping of commodities[1] in bulk[2] over land feasible for the first time in history. With the steamship, tens of millions of people could cross the oceans with ease – and did so. The first transatlantic cable was laid in 1866. This was the most important breakthrough of the last 200 years for the capital markets. No other innovation including the late nineteenth-century invention, the telephone, or its late twentieth-century equivalent, the Internet, has had comparable impact on the speed of information flows and capital market integration.
The 20th century added the container ship, the giant tanker, and the airliner. It also added radio, television, transcontinental telephony, the satellite, the computer, and the Internet. New opportunities have been created and, again, they have been exploited. They are to be seen in 24-hour financial markets, mass tourism, and the global interconnection of production that has spawned[3] the multinational corporations of today. In the long run, then, the world seems bound to become more globalised because opportunities have grown enormously.
But history tells us that this does not mean a never-ending rise in integration. In the 19th century, a rising ride of liberalism reached its highest point in the last one or two decades of the century. Thereupon a combination of powerful forces reversed the tide[4]. I define those forces as the four "Is": geopolitical insecurity – the rivalry among the great powers that culminated[5] in two world wars; macroeconomic instability – above all the Great Depression; protectionist[6] interests – particularly important in the United States in 1930; and collectivist ideas – nationalism, imperialism, socialism, and communism. By 1945, the integrated world economy had disappeared.

Find out what the four ▶ Is mean for the economic down-swing. If necessary consult an Encyclopedia or the Internet.

[1] **commodity** thing bought in a shop and put to use in the home [2] **bulk** size, quantity
[3] **to spawn** to appear in great numbers [4] **to reverse the tide** to change the trend around completely [5] **to culminate in sth.** to reach the highest point of development
[6] **protectionist** supporter of home industries

▼ **Read the following paragraphs very slowly in order to understand the new wave of liberalisation – take notes.**

After World War II, liberalisation began anew, though haltingly, in Western Europe and across the Atlantic under the wise leadership of the United States. By the late 1960s, the success of a small number of relatively outward-looking east Asian economies was becoming more visible. By the late 1970s, the failures of state planning and nationalisation were also becoming evident. This set the stage for what must be the most dramatic period of economic liberalisation there has ever been – a process that has, in a quarter of a century, brought something like four billion additional people within the purview[7] of the global market.

Think of the transformation of Mao Zedong's China into what is, almost certainly, the most internationally open large country in history; the collapse of the Soviet empire, etc. These events alone transformed the economic lives of about 2.8 billion people. But this was not all. Economic liberalisation also swept across much of Latin America.

In all these cases, moreover, what happened was not just liberalisation at the border. As has usually been the case, the move towards the market has been simultaneously[8] internal and external. There have been exceptions: The United States was one in the 19th century, when it combined high protection against imports with laissez-faire at home. But when countries decide to adopt the logic of the market, they normally do so both domestically and internationally. [...]

---

[7] **purview** the limits of sb.'s interest or activity [8] **simultaneously** at the same time

Activities

The globalisation process

1. Analyse the article by visualising it in a mind map. Use your notes.

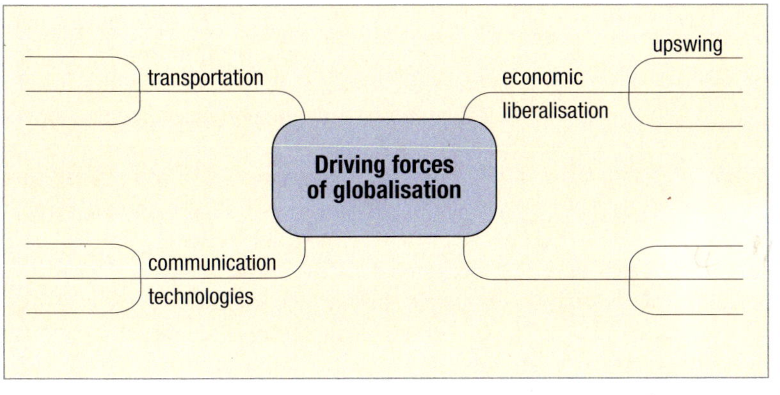

2. According to the author, four Is stopped the process of economic integration in the first decades of the 20th century. Try to explain his point of view.

3. Using your mind map, give a talk on the driving factors of globalisation.

Internal and external liberalisation

4. The last paragraph deals with domestic and international liberalisation. Paraphrase it for someone who has not read the whole article.

Open Markets – Economic Liberalisation

Open markets (international, free trade without import and export barriers) and foreign direct investment[1] (FDI) have led to deeper forms of economic interdependence[2] among nations.

- World trade is 16 times greater today than it was in 1950.
- Outflows of foreign direct investment have grown even faster, rising twenty-five fold from $14 billion to $350 billion a year.

Voices for and against economic liberalisation

Open markets rest on solid foundations. One of these is the fact that when individuals and companies engage in specialisation and exchange, a country will exploit[3] its comparative advantage. It will devote its natural, human, industrial and financial resources to their highest and best uses. This will provide gains to firms and consumers alike.
OECD

A more open domestic market is not a handicap; it is a source of competitive[4] strength. International trade is a powerful stimulus to increase efficiency. Efficiency, in turn, contributes to economic growth and rising incomes. In the last decade, countries that have been more open have achieved double the annual average growth compared to others.
OECD

The rapid opening of markets will result in unrestricted entry of competing products. This would affect domestic industries which are not mature enough to face the onslaught[5] of competition.
M. Suppermaniam

Economic liberalisation means the loss of employment, as labour intensive productions are shifted to low wage countries. This raises the risk of a political backlash against free trade and capital flows.
M. Suppermaniam

[1] **investment** the process of giving money to a company or business in order to get a profit [2] **interdependence** depending on each other [3] **to exploit** to use sth. fully and effectively [4] **competitive** *wettbewerbsbetont* [5] **onslaught** the effect of sth. that is unpleasant and could cause damage, violent attack

Activities

Open markets

1. Study the boxes and list the main points under the following headings:

Open markets/free trade	
advantages	disadvantages
....	....
....	....

Your opinion

2. In your view, what are the advantages of foreign investments?

Jeans – The Journey of Blue Jeans in a Global, Liberalised World

The map shows the long journey of jeans from the time of harvesting cotton up to the moment you can buy them.

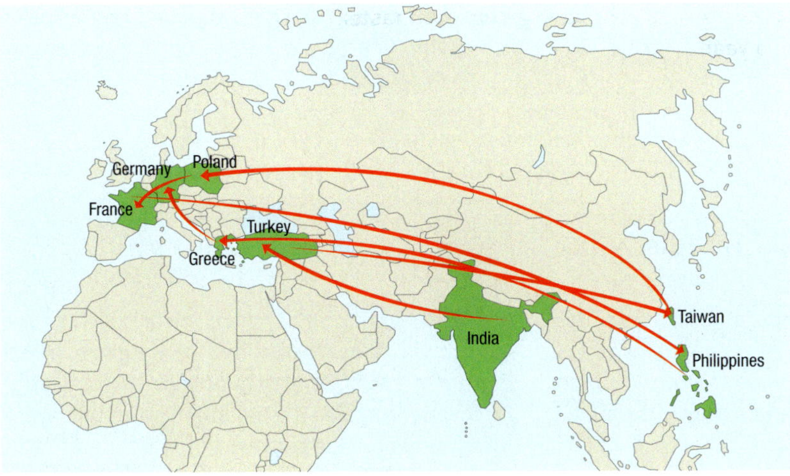

0 miles	India – Cotton is harvested.
3,000 miles	Turkey – Cotton is spun into yarn.
9,000 miles	Taiwan – Yarn is dyed with indigo from Germany.
16,000 miles	Poland – The textile is woven.
17,000 miles	France – Lining, labels and buttons are fastened.
26,000 miles	Philippines – All accessories are sewn together.
33,000 miles	Greece – treatment with pumice
35,000 miles	Germany – jeans on sale

Activities

1. The map and notes describe a rather complicated production process. What do you think of it?
2. Find out about how another product is made.

The production process

Outsourcing – Two Examples

The term **outsourcing** means the process of shifting services or the production of goods to an external company that has specialised in the respective field. This is what happens very often, e.g. when a car manufacturer has car parts produced by another firm in the home country. When the other company is located in another country the process is called **offshore outsourcing**. A special case in today's global economy is the transfer of all production to low-wage countries, mostly in Eastern Europe or Asia. Nowadays lots of large firms tend to go abroad whereas middle-sized enterprises stay in their home country.
Note that the terms *outsourcing* and *offshore outsourcing* are often used interchangeably.

Moving the Manufacture of Cleaners to Malaysia

James Dyson, the entrepreneurial[1] inventor, caused considerable controversy when he moved the manufacture of his cleaners[2] from Malmesbury to Malaysia to save costs. Four years later the move does not seem so controversial. The world is now more aware of the impact of globalisation, including the almost unlimited potential of emerging economies in Asia, and China in particular, to manufacture most of the goods we consume at much lower costs. In his lecture this week – the first to be given by an engineer – Mr Dyson was unrepentant[3]. Manufacturing costs had been going up and the prices he was able to charge were going down. He had to shift manufacturing to a low-cost area, where most of his components came from anyway, in order to save the company, which now employed more people at Malmesbury, including higher paid scientists and engineers, than before. The Dyson experience is important because many more companies, or what is left of them from Britain's shrunken manufacturing base, will face similar decisions in future unless they happen to make high-added value products such as Rolls-Royce engines that are not yet so easily replicated[4]. Gordon Brown warned last week that in addition to having very low labour costs, India and China produced more than 4mil graduates each year compared with only 250,000 in the UK. This week a Chinese company purchased the whole of IBM's personal computer activities, a prospect that would have been unthinkable 10 years ago. Yesterday, it was revealed[5] that the UK had a near-record trade deficit on goods and services in October of £3.8bn, reflecting the UK's increasing uncompetitiveness[6] as a result of globalisation and a strong pound. [...]

[1] **entrepreneurial** *unternehmerisch* [2] **cleaner = vacuum cleaner** machine that cleans floors by sucking up dirt
[3] **unrepentant** not feeling regret or sorrow for wrongdoing [4] **to replicate** to copy, to reproduce [5] **to reveal** to make known [6] **uncompetitiveness** not being competitive

TVR to Move its Production Abroad

Mark Milner

Sagaris
Few cars look as dramatic as the new Sagaris.

Tuscan S
The unique Tuscan is already a legend.

Tuscan S Convertible
Almighty Tuscan as a spectacular convertible.

The sports car maker TVR is planning to transfer production to Europe in a move that will mean the loss of up to 250 jobs, the company's Russian owner, Nicholai Smolensky, said yesterday. The news is a bitter blow to workers at the Blackpool factory, who believed the threat of closure had been lifted. The threat to the plant first emerged in April, when TVR said it needed a smaller site. Both the Transport & General Workers Union, which represents TVR employees, and senior representatives of the North West Regional Development Agency (NWRD) are holding talks with the company. The agency said it hoped to broker a deal[1] to keep production in the region. The T&G reacted angrily to news of Mr Smolensky's decision. "This is a bitter blow to Blackpool and this iconic[2] British sportscar," the Union's regional officer, Dave McCall, said. "It is hard to take in after everyone's hopes had been raised just a few months ago when workers who had been laid off were taken back."

In a statement, Mr Smolensky said that TVR planned to move all production. "Agreements are being finalised for the 2007 run of the Tuscan, Tuscan Convertible and Sagaris to be produced in Europe," he said. Production of power trains – engines, clutches and gear boxes – will remain in the UK.

The company has given no indication as to where production will be moved. But last night there was speculation that it could be to Italy, France or Eastern Europe. Mr Smolensky said: "We are extremely sorry that after a period of uncertainty and raised hopes that we could continue production ourselves in Blackpool we have had to make this decision. "We need to secure the future of the company and move forward. I am afraid we see no other way to do so."

[...]

[1] **to broker a deal** to arrange the details of sth. so that everyone can agree to it [2] **iconic** regarded as a symbol of sth.

Activities

1. Compare the Dyson and the TVR companies.

2. Due to globalisation, more and more companies shift production to low-cost countries. What are the advantages, what the disadvantages? List your ideas in a chart.

Outsourcing examples

Pros and cons

Return of a Conundrum

Jeremy Rifkin

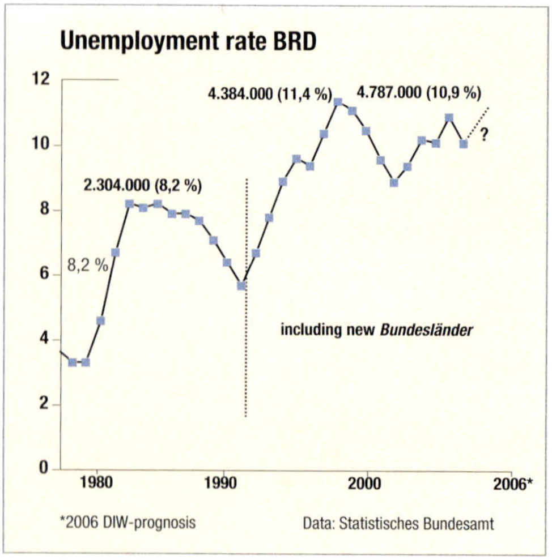

We are losing jobs all over the world. It has reached crisis proportions. In 1995, 800 million people were unemployed or under-employed. Today, more than a billion fall into one of these categories.

Even in America and Europe, millions of workers find themselves underemployed or without jobs and with little hope of obtaining full-time employment. The US has lost 12 % of its factory jobs since 1998, while the UK shed 14 % of its manufacturing jobs in the same period. Manufacturing jobs continue to disappear in the UK, even though the sector is growing at its fastestpace in four years.

Where have all the factory jobs gone? It has become fashionable, of late, to blame the high unemployment on companies relocating their production facilities to China and other countries. [...]

There's more bad news. According to Alliance Capital, 31 m manufacturing jobs were eliminated between 1995 and 2002 in the world's 20 largest economies. Manufacturing employment has declined every year in the past seven years and in every region of the world. The employment decline[1] occurred[2] during a period when global industrial production rose by more than 30 %. If the current rate of decline continues – and it is more than likely to accelerate[3] – manufacturing employment will dwindle[4] from the current 164m jobs to just a few million by 2040, virtually ending the era of mass factory labour. Now the white-collar and services industries are experiencing similar job losses, as intelligent technologies replace more and more workers. [...]

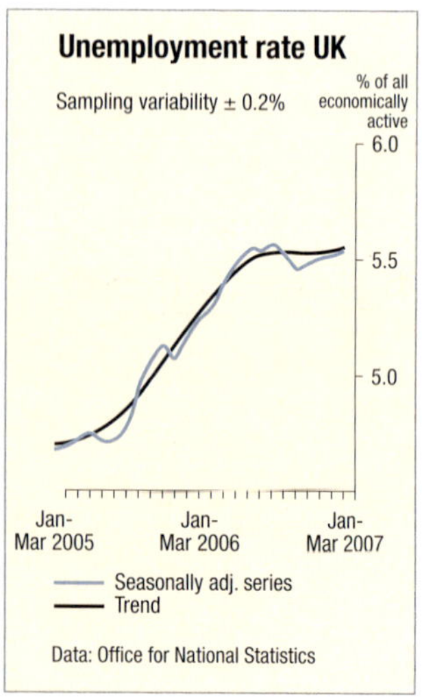

conundrum puzzling problem [1] **decline** loss of numbers [2] **to occur** to happen
[3] **to accelerate** to increase the speed [4] **to dwindle** to gradually become less and less

Activities

The job situation according to Rifkin

1. According to Rifkin, one of the effects of globalisation is an increase in redundancies. Summarise his view in key words.
2. How does Rifkin emphasise the seriousness of the situation?

The effect of unemployment

3. Industry wants to be competitive on the world market and fires employees to save production costs. What will the social impact of a steadily growing unemployment rate be?
4. Lots of young people, Germans as well as foreigners, are out of work in Germany. What do you think of their situation? What could be done about it?

Globalisation and the Developing World

Henry Ekwuruke

Some of the burning questions often asked include the following: Does economic globalisation worsen inequality of nations or could it help in the reduction of poverty? Are countries that integrate with the global economy better or worse off economically in the short or long term? Globalisation, economically speaking, involves the integration of world trade and financial markets; but given that developing countries are not really catching up with the advanced economies, the impact of globalisation on the Third World Countries leaves much to be desired.

▼ This passage deals with reasons for the economic backwardness of Third World countries. Underline key words or take notes.

[...] In the arena of world trade, the share of primary commodities[1] in world exports of items such as food and raw materials has declined relatively in recent times. In the area of capital movements, it is noticed that the net official flows of "aid" or development assistance from the advanced economies to the Third World Countries have dwindled[2] significantly since the early 1980s. [...] In the rather disturbing area of lending policies by the International Monetary Fund (IMF), for instance, it is well known that a larger chunk[3] of Nigeria's foreign debt, as a case in point, derives from the ever increasing interest-arrears and penalties[4] for non-payment. It is especially on this score that one tends to wonder if globalisation is not sometimes synonymous with economic justice?

The accusation has often been made against the IMF and the World Bank[5] as being largely responsible for the rather deplorable economic woes and backwardness of many Third World Countries, Nigeria included. [...]

A slum in Kenya

[1] **commodity** article of trade [2] **to dwindle** to become less or smaller [3] **chunk** a piece
[4] **interest-arrears and penalties** *Schuldzinsen und Vertragsstrafen* [5] **IMF (International Monetary Fund) and WB (the World Bank)** promoters of globalisation who provide loans to poor countries

Read the following ▼ passage carefully sentence by sentence and find out what the author means by "a new culture of solidarity and justice".

The African youth must call for the people in the West to continue to develop in the current process of globalisation forms of cooperation which are not merely economic but social and cultural as well – rethinking international cooperation in terms of a new culture of solidarity and justice. Technology-advanced and richer nations should promote and implement[6] globalisation in solidarity of the values of equity, freedom and justice, based on the firm conviction that the global marketplace needs to be appropriately controlled by the forces of society and by the state, so as to guarantee that the basic needs of the whole society are satisfied. Globalisation, when not carried out in the right spirit of humane solidarity, could very easily become a mega bombshell of exploitation of the already economically, technologically and socially disadvantaged Third World countries. And this, history sadly shows that the lending policies of the IMF and the World Bank as well as the modus operandi[7] of many multinationals have often plunged[8] the Third World Countries into deeper economic crises than ever before. [...]

Understand the ▶ lending schemes of monetary organisations and countries.

In this regard, strong voices have been raised in recent times, calling for debt relief[9] or even the total cancellation[10] of the debts of the poorest of the developing countries. Such clarion[11] calls have incidentally not fallen on deaf ears, as the IMF and the World Bank have jointly agreed to write off some debts, circa $ USD 27 billion owed them by the poorest countries of the Third World. However, even after the cancellation of the debts owed to the IMF and World Bank, some Third World Countries (like Mali and some others in the sub-Saharan region) would still have to grapple with[12] some other enormous bilateral debts from low interest loans that have been given them as foreign aid by Japan, France and the like. [...]

There are risks ▼ associated with the globalisation process in Third World countries. Underline key words.

Concluding, globalisation may well have the potential of making Third World Countries grow economically, technologically, educationally, politically and otherwise stronger. However, it is no secret that there are several risks ingrained[13] in it which at one point or the other, tend to turn one or the other Third World country into the Third of the Third World if due care is not taken! Granted that democracy (which has now come to stay in many Third World countries) ensures the recognition of human rights and the administration of justice, there are oftentimes certain dictates due to globalisation of world economy which descend on Third World countries like unjust economic plagues. Indeed many a conditionality[14] of the IMF or the World Bank's lending schemes would hardly be seen as promoting the dignity and fundamental rights of the inhabitants of the southern hemisphere who are constrained[15], due to harsh economic policies, exchange adverse[16] rates and other aberrations[17] in the world market place to seek loans from these international monetary organisations, who instead of ameliorating[18] the economic woes of the borrowers, end up adding insult to injury by the way borrowers are made to cough out the ever amassing interests on the loans! It is indeed an open secret that most often the structural reforms that the lending organisations (IMF and the World Bank) ask

The **Heavily Indebted Poor Countries (HIPC)** Initiative was first started in 1996 by the IMF and World Bank, with the aim of ensuring that no poor country faces a debt burden it cannot manage. In 1999, a number of modifications were approved to provide faster, deeper, and broader debt relief and to strengthen the links between debt relief, poverty reduction, and social policies. In 2005, the HIPC Initiative was enlarged by the Multilateral Debt Relief Initiative (MDRI) which allows for 100 percent relief by three multilateral institutions: the IMF, the International Development Association (IDA) of the World Bank, and the African Development Fund (AfDF).

---

[6] **to implement** to carry sth. out [7] **modus operandi** *Verfahrensweise* [8] **to plunge** to push or dive deep into sth. [9] **debt relief** *Schuldenerlass* [10] **cancellation** giving up a planned activity [11] **clarion** clear, loud [12] **to grapple with sth.** *sich mit etwas herumschlagen* [13] **ingrained** fixed formly [14] **conditionality** *Bedingtheit* [15] **constrained** forced to do sth. [16] **adverse** *widrig* [17] **aberration** departing from the rule [18] **to ameliorate** to make better

Protesting against exploitation and poverty at the World Social Forum in Kenya, 2007

the borrowing nations to embark upon[19] do actually aggravate[20] their poverty!

Finally, and as a summary, globalisation put in balance, is a welcome development for the contemporary world (a world which due to improved information and communications technology facilities is often described as a planetary village), but a lot still has to be done, especially in the sphere of the IMF and the World Bank's lending policies to help rather than hamper[21] economic prosperity particularly to Third World nations.

[19] **to embark upon** to accept [20] **to aggravate** to make worse [21] **to hamper** to hinder sth.

Activities

Globalisation and Third World countries

1. Summarise the author's view about the impact of globalisation on developing countries in two or three sentences.
2. What does he especially deplore?
3. What should remedial measures include?

The author's strategy

4. How does the author try to win our support for his views?

Your opinion

5. How could the situation, demonstrated in the cartoon, be improved? Design a leaflet.

Kenya: Focus on Working Conditions in EPZ Companies

The impact of globalisation on Third World Countries leaves much to be desired. The following article describes labour conditions in a factory where clothes are produced for the international market.

While reading the ▼ article take notes of the labour conditions in EPZ factories.

A garment factory in Africa

Inside a typical EPZ[1] garment[2] factory, the machine operators, helpers and quality controllers work while sitting or standing for between eight and 12 hours daily, with only a 45-minute break in between, in order to fulfil the quota set by the supervisors. Their daily pay is between US $1.90 and $2.20, but a percentage is deducted[3] for social security or hospital insurance contributions[4], which rarely benefit them. Often, the machines get hot and, without ventilation, the workers are constantly in a state of extreme discomfort. The story is similar in the food industry, where few workers are enrolled in health schemes[5], and have hardly any savings. There are cases in which workers, especially pregnant women, have collapsed or fallen seriously ill after long hours of hard work. [...]

Janet, a helper in a garment factory in Nairobi's Ruaraka area, said she sometimes works around the clock, with only short breaks. "If you don't meet your target, you will be detained[6] inside the factory even if it means working until morning," she said.

Other female EPZ workers tell even more depressing tales of verbal and sexual violence they suffer at the hands of their "masters", including rape[7] and beatings. [...]

In a new report on EPZs in Kenya, the KHRC[8] said labour conditions in EPZs reflected the worst effects of globalisation, which, contrary to their objective of empowerment[9], end up becoming "factories for the manufacture of poverty".

As happened in other Third World countries, said the report, entitled "Manufacturing poverty: The story of EPZs in Kenya", EPZs were partly products of globalisation and partly those of donor conditionalities[10] which had forced the Kenyan government to adopt legislative measures to liberalise the economy as a means of attracting foreign investment. [...]

Cheap labour had created a situation where workers' rights were sacrificed by way of official acknowledge-

---

[1] **EPZ** Export Processing Zone that Third World Countries set up as industrial parks to make mass production of export goods easier for the international market [2] **garment** article of clothing [3] **to deduct** to take away [4] **contribution** sth. that you give [5] **to be enrolled in health schemes** to be medically insured [6] **to detain** to keep back, to prevent from leaving [7] **rape** crime of forcing sb. to have sex [8] **KHRC** Kenya Human Rights Commission, a non-profit making and non-governmental organisation [9] **empowerment** giving power to sb. [10] **donor conditionalities** *Bedingungen der Geberländer*

ment of "minimum" as opposed to "living" wages, the report added.

"Factories seek a workforce that will produce optimal results, hence the preference for young, unattached[11] women who will not only easily give in to work-based exploitation but also accept low pay without undue fuss[12]," the report states [...] "The wages are insufficient for even basic needs, forcing them into sexual relationships with their superiors or into such measures as skipping meals[13] and sharing tiny rooms," the report said. [...]

A global campaign being carried out by various NGOs[14] targets[15], mainly big food and clothing retailers[16], who are regarded as the worst culprits[17] responsible for depressing employment conditions in EPZs for millions of women workers around the world.

By using their power at the top of global supply chains[18] to squeeze[19] their suppliers to deliver, the companies deny millions of women of their fair share of benefits of globalisation by transferring the pressure on women workers in the form of longer hours at faster work rates, with poor pay, campaigners say.

A flea market for second-hand clothes in Kenya

According to Gerard Steehouwer, the growth of EPZs and violation of workers' rights around the world are symptoms of the same disease – the neoliberal economic model focusing on net exports, in which governments are forced to compete with one another in offering an easy investment climate[20]. With more than 3,000 EPZs in 100 countries around the world, major brand companies and supermarket chains had a wide range of choice in goods such as textiles and farm products from Third World countries, which helped drive down their buying prices and increase their profit margins. This stiff competition squeezed factory owners, who in turn were forced to pay poor wages to reduce the cost of production, he added. "These brand companies are squeezing out local producers, who in turn squeeze their workers." [...]

[11] **unattached** not married [12] **fuss** *Aufregung* [13] **to skip meals** to leave out meals [14] **NGO** non-governmental organisation [15] **to target** to attack, to criticise [16] **retailer** *Einzelhändler* [17] **culprit** person who has done wrong [18] **supply chain** *Handelskette* [19] **to squeeze** *unter Druck setzen* [20] **investment climate** *Investitionsbedingungen*

Activities

Labour conditions in EPZs

1. Describe the working conditions in EPZ's garment factories.
2. Who is responsible for the depressing employment conditions?
3. What part does the process of globalisation play?

The journalist speaks

4. Which words and expressions in the article stress the workers' situation?

How to improve conditions

5. How could labour conditions in EPZ companies be improved? Write a letter to the KHRC and make a suggestion.

Globalisation is an Anomaly and its Time is Running Out

James Howard Kunstler

Try to find out why the ▼ author thinks globalisation has come to an end.

Today's transient[1] global economic relations are a product of very special transient circumstances, namely relative world peace and absolutely reliable supplies of cheap energy. Subtract either of these elements from the equation[2] and you will see globalisation evaporate[3] so quickly it will suck the air out of your lungs. It is significant that none of the cheerleaders for globalisation takes this equation into account. In fact, the American power elite is sleepwalking into a crisis so severe that the blowback may put both major political parties out of business.

The world saw an earlier phase of robust global trade run from the 1870s to a dead stop in 1914. This was the boom period of railroad construction and the advent of the ocean-going steamship. The great powers had existed in relative peace since Napoleon's last stand. [...]

Norwegian oil-rig

There was no shortage of fuel[4], the colonial boundaries were stable and the pipeline of raw materials from them to the factories of western Europe ran smoothly. The rise of a middle class running the many stages of the production process provided markets for all the new production. Innovations in finance gave legitimacy to all kinds of tradable paper[5]. Life was very good for Europe and America, notwithstanding[6] a few sharp cyclical depressions and recoveries. Trade boomed between the great powers. In America, it was called the progressive era. The 20th century looked golden.

It all fell apart in 1914 [...] and a new round of globalisation did not ramp[7] up again until the mid-1960s. It may be significant that the first collapse of globalisation occurred as the coal economy was transitioning[8] into an oil economy, with deep geo-political implications[9] for who had oil (America) and those who might seek to control the other major region closest to Europe that possessed it (then the Caspian, since Arabian oil was as yet undiscovered). The first world war was settled by those nations (Britain and France) that were friendly with the greatest producer of oil

[1] **transient** lasting only for a short time [2] **equation** *Gleichgewicht* [3] **to evaporate** to disappear [4] **fuel** wood, coal, oil, etc. that you burn to make heat or power [5] **tradable papers** shares, bonds, etc., which you can buy and sell [6] **notwithstanding** in spite of [7] **to ramp up** here: to start again [8] **to transition** to change [9] **implication** a suggestion not expressed but understood

most readily accessed[10]. Germany was the loser and again in the reprise[11] for its poor access to oil.
Japan suffered similarly. We are now due for another folding up of the periodical global trade fair as the industrial nations enter the tumultuous era beyond the global oil production peak[12], which I have named the long emergency[13]. The economic distortions[14] and perversities built up in the current era are not hard to see, though our leaders dread[15] to acknowledge them. The dirty secret of the US economy for at least a decade now is that it has come to be based on the ceaseless elaboration[16] of a car-dependent suburban infrastructure – McHousing estates, eight-lane highways, big-box chain stores, hamburger stands – that has no future as a living arrangement in an oil-short future.

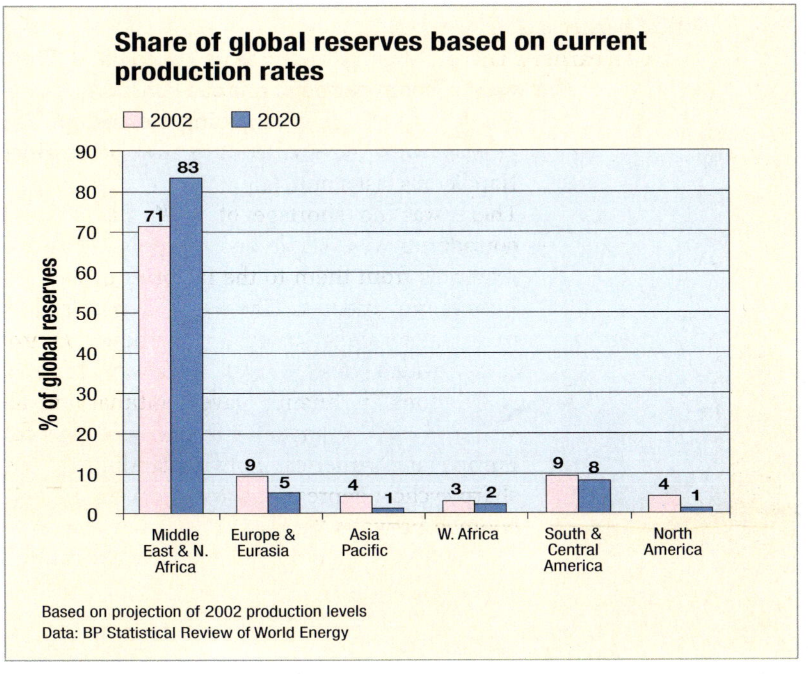

The American suburban juggernaut[17] can be described succinctly[18] as the greatest misallocation[19] of resources in the history of the world. The mortgages, bonds, real estate investment trusts and derivative financial instruments[20] associated with this tragic enterprise must make the judicious[21] goggle[22] with wonder and nausea[23]. Add to this grim economic picture a far-flung military contest, already under way, really, for control of the world's remaining oil, and the scene grows darker.

---

[10] **to access** easy to use [11] **reprise** *Wiederkehr* [12] **peak** highest point [13] **emergency** serious and dangerous situation [14] **distortion** changing the appearance of sth.
[15] **to dread** to be afraid of sth. [16] **elaboration** careful realisation [17] **juggernaut** very large lorry [18] **succinctly** clearly expressed in a few words [19] **misallocation** *Fehlanlage*
[20] **mortgages, bonds, real estate investment trusts and derivative financial instruments** *Hypotheken, Verpflichtungen, Grundstücksinvestitionskonzerne und sekundäre Finanzapparate*
[21] **judicious** having good judgement [22] **to goggle** to look with your eyes wide open
[23] **nausea** feeling and desire to vomit

Sheikh al-Sabah, Prince Abdel Asis and Sheikh Hamad el Thani opening the OPEC-conference in Caracas (Sept. 27, 2000)

Two-thirds of that oil is in the possession of people who resent[24] the West (America in particular), many of whom have vowed to destroy it. Both America and Britain have felt the sting of war-makers not associated with a particular state but with a transnational religious cause that uses potent small arms and explosives to unravel[25] western societies and confound[26] their defences. China, a supposed beneficiary[27] of globalisation, will be as desperate for oil as all the other players, and perhaps more ruthless[28] in seeking control of the supplies, some of which they can walk to. Of course, it is hard to imagine the continuation of American chain stores' manufacturing supply lines with China, given the potential for friction. Even on its own terms, China faces issues of environmental havoc[29], population overshoot, and political turmoil – orders of magnitude greater than anything known in Europe or America. Viewed through this lens, the sunset of the current phase of globalisation seems dreadfully close to the horizon. The American public has enjoyed the fiesta, but the blue-light special orgy of easy motoring, limitless air-conditioning, and super-cheap products made by factory slaves far far away is about to close down. Globalisation is finished.

---

[24] **to resent** to feel angry or bitter at [25] **to unravel** to separate [26] **to confound** to confuse [27] **beneficiary** sb. who gets advantage from an action or change [28] **ruthless** showing no human feelings [29] **havoc** disorder

Activities

Globalisation in the course of time

1. What are – according to the author – the fundamental elements of globalisation?
2. How does he judge the two main phases of globalisation?
3. How does he justify his thesis that globalisation is finished?

Author and text

4. Which words and expressions stress Kunstler's view?

Your emotional response

5. How do you see Kunstler's theory that globalisation is finished?

Global Challenges – What Politics and Organisations Can Do

The phenomenon of globalisation is not limited to the economic and socio-cultural spheres but also has a political-institutional dimension. The problems of this world have become global challenges and cannot be solved by individual nation states any more but demand multi-lateral responses either by individual statesmen or by supra-national institutions like the UN, WTO, etc.

Only a limited number of problems can be dealt with in this unit. Those that have been chosen are of particular relevance today: Global warming, poverty, terrorism, and peace.

"It's Global Warming, Stupid!"

One can no longer deny the fact that something has occurred and is occurring to our climate. The signs of a warming world are there for everybody to see, hear, and feel. Global temperatures and sea levels seem to be rising, causing havoc to the world's weather and destruction to various countries.

Global warming does not necessarily mean that all regions of our planet warm up. In fact, some regions may even cool a little. Global warming is generally attributed to the effect of human-generated carbon dioxide and other gases being released into our planet's atmosphere. Mankind is to blame. The industrial nations are the main perpetrators – with the USA and China being the biggest polluters, but developing countries are responsible as well.

The following texts deal with effects and causes of this phenomenon and discuss possible solutions.

Review of the End of the World News

Martin Rowson

Activities

Analysing the cartoon

1. Describe what you can see in the foreground, centre and background.
2. What problems/issues does the cartoonist allude to? What does he criticise? What is his message?
3. What satirical devices does the cartoonist use?

Your opinion

4. Do you think the cartoonist achieves his aim?

End of the World Nigh – It's Official

Michael Meacher

▼ **Focus on the author's main arguments.**

There is a lot wrong with our world. But it is not as bad as many people think. It is worse. Global warming is slowly but relentlessly[1] changing the face of the planet.

We are only in the early stages of this process, but already carbon dioxide in the atmosphere has reached 375 parts per million, the highest level for at least half a million years. Temperatures are projected to rise up to 5.8°C this century, ten times the increase of 0.6°C in the last century, and 40% more than this in some northern land surface areas. This means temperatures could rise by 8.1°C in some parts of the world.

Does this matter? The evidence suggests that it does. In China severe[2] floods used to occur once every 20 years; now they occur in nine out of every 10. The number of people affected by floods globally has risen from 7 million in the 1960s to 150 million now. In 1998 two-thirds of Bangladesh was under water for months, affecting 30 million people. In the UK, 5 million people and 185,000 businesses are at risk.

Flooding is only the beginning. The number of people worldwide devastated[3] by hurricanes or cyclones has increased eightfold to 25 million a year over the past 30 years. The oceans are steadily warming, and since they currently absorb 50 times more CO_2 than is contained in the atmosphere, even a tiny reduction in CO_2 absorption by the sea could cause global temperatures to rise significantly.

Even more seriously, 10,000 billion tonnes of methane (a greenhouse gas 20 times more potent than CO_2) are stored, according to US Geological Survey, on the shallow[4] floor of the arctic, in sediments below the seabed. If the temperature surrounding the methane warms, it becomes unstable[5] and methane gas is released[6] causing temperatures to increase further. Warming oceans also cause the waters to expand and sea level to rise. Sea level is predicted to rise by 3ft over the next century, leading to huge areas of Bangladesh, Egypt and China being inundated[7].

We don't know the limits of nature – how much rain could fall for how long a period, how much more powerful and frequent hurricanes could become, for how long droughts[8] could endure[9]. The ultimate concern is that if runaway global warming occurred, temperatures could spiral[10] out of control and make our planet uninhabitable[11].

Five times in the past 540 million years there have been mass extinctions, in one case involving the destruction of 90% of species then living. But while these were the result of asteroid strikes[12] or intense glaciation[13], this is the first time that a species has been at risk of generating its own demise[14]. [...]

---

[1] **relentless** constant [2] **severe** extreme, very bad [3] **to devastate** to ruin [4] **shallow** not deep [5] **unstable** likely to change suddenly [6] **to release** to set free [7] **to inundate** to flood a place [8] **drought** long period of time during which no rain falls [9] **to endure** to continue [10] **to spiral** *hochschnellen* [11] **uninhabitable** not fit to live in [12] **asteroid strike** sudden hit by a small planet [13] **glaciation** process in which land is covered by glaciers [14] **demise** death

Polar bear – an endangered species

We have almost become our geophysical cycle[15]. There are many examples of this trend. On a global scale[16] our biological Carbon productivity is now only outpaced[17] by the krill[18] in the oceans. Our civil engineering works[19] shift more soil than the world's rivers bring to the seas. Our industrial emissions eclipse[20] the total emissions from all the world's volcanoes. We are bringing about[21] species loss on the scale of some of the natural extinctions of palaeohistory[22]. [...]
The dinosaurs dominated the earth for 160 million years. We are in danger of putting our future at risk after a mere quarter of a million years. [...]
The lesson is that if we continue with activities which destroy our environment and undermine[23] the conditions for our own survival, we are the virus. Making the change needed to avoid that fate[24] is perhaps the greatest challenge we have ever faced.

---

[15] **geophysical cycle** *geophysikalischer Kreislauf* [16] **scale** *Skala* [17] **to outpace** to out do [18] **krill** tiny shellfish [19] **civil engineering works** *Hoch- und Tiefbau* [20] **to eclipse** to make unimportant [21] **to bring about** to make sth. happen [22] **palaeohistory** history relating to the early part of the Stone Age [23] **to undermine** make weaker at the base [24] **fate** destiny

Activities

Reasons and effects of global warming

1. Make a list of the author's main arguments so that you understand his message.
2. Draw two different graphs using coordinate axes to visualise the effects of global warming on the rise of temperatures and on the number of people affected by floods globally.
3. Apart from the effects of global warming Meacher points out there are others he does not mention or expand upon:
   a) the meltdown of the earth's ice cover: the meltdown of the polar ice/the ice melt in Greenland/the meltdown and retreat of glaciers all over the world,
   b) the extinction of terrestrial species: land animals and plants/the coral crisis,
   c) changing weather patterns: the increase in numbers and strength of hurricanes, cyclones, flooding of islands and coasts.

   Find out more details about these effects of global warming. Use the Internet or other publications to collect information and prepare a presentation.

The author's strategies

4. Do you think Meacher's "End-of-the-world" scenario is convincing? What strategies does he use to convince his readers?

A hot seat discussion

5. This article was based on a lecture Meacher delivered at Newcastle University. Imagine you are Michael Meacher and that you had delivered the lecture. Now, slip into his role, sit down on a chair in front of the class, and let your classmates ask you about your lecture.

The Kyoto Protocol – The Background

Craig Donnellan

Global warming has become one of the central issues in the context of the globalisation debate. Attempts at combating it have been made at various conferences beginning in the 1970s. The most famous and much publicized conference at Kyoto, Japan, in 1997 resulted in the Kyoto Protocol. The deal originally included 38 of the world's most developed nations and has in the meantime been signed by 169 states.
The most recent attempt at curbing greenhouse gas emissions made at the UN climate change conference in Nairobi (November 2006) ended with little results. 180 countries agreed to review the Kyoto Protocol in 2008. The USA and Australia are not among them. They show hardly any inclination to change their attitudes and sign a successor agreement, when the Kyoto Protocol runs out in 2012. Neither do China and India.

▼ **Concentrate on the agreements at the "Earth Summit" at Rio de Janeiro and at the Kyoto Conference.**

The United Nations Framework Convention on Climate Change (UNFCCC) was signed by the overwhelming majority of world leaders at the 'Earth Summit' in Rio de Janeiro in 1992. In the UNFCCC, which came into force in 1994, contracting countries all agree (in Article Two) to 'achieve stabilisation of greenhouse gas concentrations in the atmosphere at a level that would prevent dangerous anthropogenic[1] interference with the climate system [...] within a time frame sufficient to allow ecosystems to adapt naturally to climate change, to ensure that food production is not threatened, and to enable economic development to proceed[2] in a suitable manner.'

Developed nations (those of the OECD[3] and the former Warsaw Pact) were also committed to reduce their emissions of greenhouse gases in 2000 to the 1990 level.

Further targets for the control of greenhouse gases were agreed at the third conference of the parties to the convention at Kyoto, Japan, in 1997, giving rise to the Kyoto Protocol. This requires developed countries to reduce their annual emissions of greenhouse gases by (on average) 5.2 per cent from the 1990 level by 2008–2012. The EU undertook to achieve an 8 per cent reduction, within which the UK is required to cut emissions by 12,5 per cent.

A key part of the Kyoto Protocol is that some of the emission reductions required of developed countries may be met by transferring reductions in emissions across national boundaries, under the so-called 'flexibility mechanisms' (FMs). These take three forms:

- Emissions Trading – a developed country that has exceeded[4] its Kyoto targets to reduce carbon dioxide emissions can sell its surplus[5] reduction to another developed country that has failed to meet its target.

---

[1] **anthropogenic** caused by human beings [2] **to proceed** to continue [3] **OECD** Organisation for Economic Co-operation and Development [4] **to exceed** to go over [5] **surplus** excess

- Joint Implementation[6] – a developed country can fund a project in another developed country that will either reduce carbon dioxide emissions (such as improving the efficiency of a power station), or enhance[7] carbon 'sinks'[8] (such as TEPCO's[9] carbon forestry in Tasmania). The reduction of carbon dioxide in the atmosphere is allocated[10] to the country financing the project.
- Clean Development Mechanism – a developed country can fund a project in an underdeveloped country that will either reduce carbon dioxide emissions, or enhance carbon 'sinks'. Such projects must produce 'reductions in emissions that are additional to any that would occur in the absence of a certified[11] project activity'. [...]

---

[6] **implementation** putting into action [7] **to enhance** to improve [8] **carbon sink** carbon reservoir, based on the natural ability of trees and other plants to store carbon [9] **TEPCO** Tokyo Electric Power Company [10] **to allocate** to give [11] **to certify** to declare as true

Activities

Solutions

1. What were the most important agreements at the "Earth Summit" in Rio de Janeiro and at the conference in Kyoto?
2. Explain the different aspects of the FMs (Flexibility Mechanisms).
3. The following newspaper headlines refer to other possible solutions to the problem of global warming. Discuss which solutions the headlines refer to.

Wind power use grows by 30 %
(New York Times, 2002)

Nuclear plants blooming
(Guardian Weekly, 2004)

Burying Carbon
(The Guardian, 2005)

Saving the rain-forest
(The Economist, 2004)

Green claims for hybrid cars fail to add up, says *Which?* survey
(The Guardian, 2006)

4. What is your opinion of the Kyoto Protocol and other possible solutions to the problem of global warming?

Writing and debating exercise

5. Write a short essay on any of the solutions mentioned above stating your point of view.
6. Prepare a debate between representatives of the industrialised and developing countries about solutions to the challenge of climate change.

Take Personal Action to Reduce Emissions

Mark Lynas

▼ While reading mark all the actions suggested by Lynas to reduce emissions.

It's easy – and in many ways justified – to blame Bush and the oil companies for causing and perpetuating[1] climate change. But we all have a role to play in reducing emissions by altering the way we live our lives. Current UK per capita[2] emissions total 9.6 tonnes of carbon dioxide a year, whereas a 'sustainable'[3] per person quota has been calculated at 2.45 tonnes. In other words we Western consumers on average need to reduce our emissions to less than a quarter of their current levels.

It sounds impossible, but relatively painless (and often beneficial) shifts in life style can make this target more than attainable[4] for the average British person. More than half of the UK's current emissions come from sectors of the economy where consumers play a direct role, from cars to kettles[5].

Space[6] heating consumes half of domestic energy use – and can be easily reduced by extra insulation[7], double-glazed[8] windows and a good-quality gas boiler. A draughty[9], badly-insulated Victorian house can take five times as much energy to heat as a fully-insulated modern house. Insulation is a low-cost, one-off[10] investment (which may also pay for itself through lower bills) and a surprising amount of financial assistance is available through a variety of little-advertised government schemes, especially for those on a low income.

It's also now fairly cheap and easy for UK consumers to change to green electricity, which means you can use market forces to help expand the renewables sector at little more than the flick of a switch[11].

Transport is still the fastest-growing contributor to global warming. Anyone who drives their car more than 10,000 miles a year will probably have already used more than double their sustainable carbon budget. The alternatives here are simple: reduce car use, switch to foot or bicycle for shorter journeys, and buses or trains for longer ones.

[1] **to perpetuate** to cause to continue [2] **per capita** per each person [3] **sustainable** maintainable [4] **attainable** achievable [5] **kettle** *(Wasser)kessel* [6] **space** area, room [7] **insulation** *Isolierung* [8] **double-glazed** with two sheets of glass [9] **draughty** air blowing through [10] **one-off** happening once [11] **flick of a switch** *Kinderspiel*

For most city-dwellers, cars are an unnecessary luxury, and hinder the development and operation of public transport. Sometimes having access to a car is very useful: perhaps to carry heavy goods around, or for occasional travel into rural areas. I had to hire one to get to the floods in Wales in a hurry, but a cheaper option is to join a car-share scheme[12], which enables many people to pool their costs into[13] one vehicle.
Aircraft are much, much worse. [...] The warming effects of the actual carbon emissions from a jet engine are tripled because of vapour contrails[14] and the fact that pollutants[15] are injected high up into the Earth's atmosphere, where they can do the most damage. [...]
Unfortunately a barrage[16] of airline advertising seeks to obscure[17] these realities, whilst I don't think I've ever seen a single advert singing the praises of continental train travel. More importantly, price incentives[18] also work the other way round: it's far cheaper to fly from London to Edinburgh than use a train, because the effects of pollution are not factored into[19] the cost of a ticket, and air transport currently enjoys a whole multitude of hidden subsidies – including, remarkably, tax-free fuel. The air industry expends a huge amount of time and money lobbying government to ensure these subsidies are protected, and that passenger numbers continue to rise unchecked.
The recent proliferation[20] of budget airlines has made the situation immeasurably worse, and the government in Britain is considering building airports and runways at several sites throughout the Southeast of England. This is the reverse of what needs to happen: demand management must be employed to reduce incentives to fly and to increase incentives for surface transport. Short-haul[21] flights can and should be phased out altogether. As the old Chinese proverb goes: it's okay to take a step backward when you're standing on the edge of a cliff.

---

[12] **scheme** clever plan [13] **to pool costs into** to share costs for [14] **vapour contrails** *Kondensstreifen* [15] **pollutant** substance that pollutes [16] **barrage** a lot of [17] **to obscure** to hide [18] **incentive** sth. that encourages you [19] **to be factored into** to be included in [20] **proliferation** very fast growth [21] **short-haul** short distance

Activities

The author's suggestions

1. What does Lynas suggest to reduce emissions?

Your opinion

2. Comment on the old Chinese proverb.
3. What obstacles are there that prevent the realisation of his suggestions?
4. How realistic are Lynas's suggestions? Why do people fail to act accordingly?

A questionaire in school

5. Prepare and carry out a survey in your school to find out about what your fellow students know about the effects of global warming and the measures suggested to combat them and whether they have done or are doing anything about it. You should prepare at least 5 questions. Present and discuss your findings in class.

Rich Man, Poor Man, Beggar Man ... – Poverty

Whenever people live in conditions of need they live in poverty. They might be in need of food, sanitation, shelter and clothes or they suffer from cold, dampness and diseases they cannot address. Most frequently they are afflicted by any number of these scourges.
Poverty has become a global problem. One sixth of humanity lives in extreme poverty (about 1.3 billion of 6.3). People living in developing countries are most often affected. The majority of people in Africa and on the Indian subcontinent are poor. Sub-Saharan Africa is the most severely affected area in the world. In Latin America about 50% of the people live in poverty.
The situation of the poor countries has not improved in recent years, rather the opposite. Poor countries have become poorer and rich countries richer. Economic globalisation has been blamed for this development. In poor countries there is no money available to invest in education, exploration, research, and innovations. So one of the preconditions for economic growth – the invention of patent-protected products – is left to the developed countries. For that reason global trade has never been equal, and free trade has never been fair.

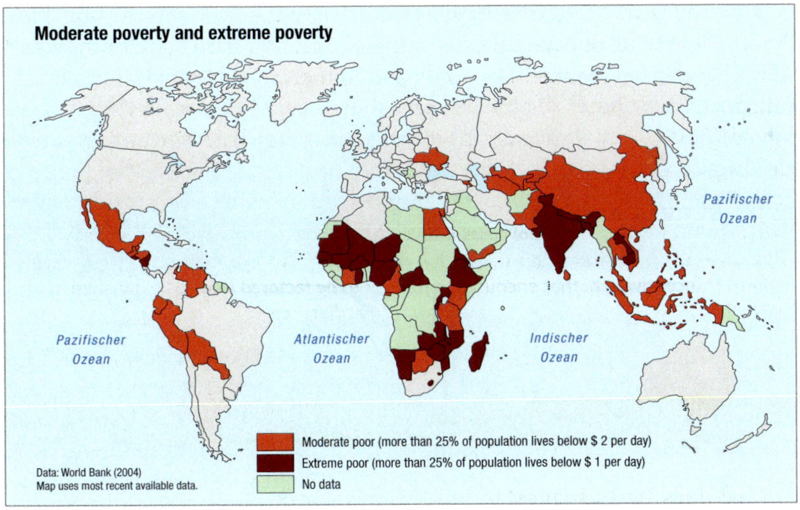

Living in Poverty – Dying of AIDS

Jeffrey D. Sachs

Sub-Saharan people have been particularly affected by poverty – for different reasons. The text refers to the situation of the inhabitants of Nthandire, Malawi.

It is still midmorning in Malawi when we arrive at a small village, Nthandire, about an hour outside of Lilongwe, the capital. We have come over dirt roads, passing women and children walking barefoot with water jugs, fuel

▼ Pay special attention to the reasons that contribute to the poverty of the villagers.

Grandmother with her grandchildren orphaned by AIDS

wood, and other bundles. The midmorning temperature is sweltering[1]. In this subsistence[2] maize-growing region of an impoverished landlocked country in southern Africa, households eke out[3] survival from an unforgiving terrain. This year has been a lot more difficult than usual because the rains have failed, probably the result of an El Niño[4] cycle. Whatever the cause, the crops[5] are withering[6] in the fields that we pass.
If the village were filled with able-bodied men who could have built small-scale water harvesting units on rooftops and in the fields to collect what little rain had fallen in the preceding months, the situation would not be as dire[7] as it is this morning. But as we arrive in the village, we see no able-bodied young men at all. In fact, older women and dozens of children greet us, but there is not a young man or woman in sight. Where, we asked, are the workers? Out in the fields? The aid worker who has led us to the village shakes his head sadly and says no. They are nearly all dead. The village has been devastated[8] by AIDS, which has ravaged[9] this part of Malawi for several years now. There are just five men between twenty and forty years of age left in the village. They are not there this morning because they are all attending the funeral of a fellow villager who died of AIDS the day before.
The presence of death in Nthandire has been overwhelming in recent years. The grandmothers whom we meet are guardians for their orphaned grandchildren. Each woman has her own story of how her sons and daughters have died, leaving her to bear the burden of raising and providing for five or ten, sometimes fifteen, orphaned grandchildren. These women have reached an age where, in more prosperous places, they would be the revered[10] matriarchs enjoying a well-earned rest from a lifetime of toil[11]. But there is no break now, no chance for even a moment's respite, because the grandmothers of this village, and countless others like it, know that if they let up for a moment, these children would die. [...]
As we proceed through the village, other grandmothers have similar stories. Each has lost sons and daughters; those that remain fight for survival. There are only poor in this village. No clinic nearby. No safe water source. No crops in the fields. And notably, no aid. I stoop down to ask one of the girls her name and age. She looks about seven or eight, but is actually twelve, stunted[12] from years of undernutrition. When I ask her what her dreams are for her own life, she says that she wants to be a teacher, and that she is prepared to study and work hard to achieve that. I know her chances of surviving to go on to secondary school and a teacher's college are slim under the circumstances in which she lives. Attending school now is a hit-

---

[1] **to be sweltering** to be hot and humid [2] **subsistance** minimum for existence [3] **to eke out** to manage [4] **El Niño** major temperature changes in surface waters of the tropical Eastern Pacific Ocean; effects on climate: rainfalls in dry areas and lack of rainfalls in areas of the east Pacific [5] **crop** what you harvest [6] **to wither** to dry up [7] **dire** dreadful [8] **devastated** ruined [9] **to ravage** to badly damage [10] **to revere** to admire and respect [11] **toil** hard, unpleasant work [12] **stunted** unable to grow

and-miss affair. Children are in and out of school with illness. Their attendance depends on how urgently they are needed at home to fetch water and firewood, or to care for siblings[13] or cousins; on whether they can afford to buy supplies, a uniform, and pay local fees, and on the safety of walking several kilometers to school itself.

[13] **sibling** brother or sister

Activities

1. Summarise the reasons that contribute to the poverty of the villagers.

The villagers

2. What is the effect of the text on the reader? How does the writer achieve this effect?

3. Invent a leaflet for the general public to be informed about the situation of the people in Nthandire, also containing a request for help to address their plight.

How to help poor people

4. What can be done about poverty globally? How can it be ended? Use the Internet to find out about the solutions suggested.
   Prepare a presentation of your findings stating your point of view.

Research on the Internet

Confronting Poverty

In Kenya, a potentially rich country, 56 percent of the population live in poverty. Its government is corrupt, its capital, Nairobi, is a city of crime.

▼ Find out what is meant by "a better way of doing things".

But far from the noise, pollution and public and private crooks[1] of Nairobi, the village of Sauri, practically on the equator, is an example of a better way of doing things. It is one of two test cases for the United Nations' ambitious program to cut poverty in half by 2015. Sauri's story shows how direct aid can largely bypass governments, getting money and help straight into the hands of the people who not only need it the most, but also know what to do with it.

Anne Omolo, the head teacher of Sauri's sole[2] primary school, arrived six years ago to find a student population that was listless[3], miserable and performing poorly in national exams. Some 500 children were enrolled, but attendance was low. She soon realized the problem. "They were hungry," she said.

So on her own, she started a food program. She went to the village parents who could afford it and asked them to bring corn and beans. But almost half of the school's students were orphans whose parents had died of AIDS,

[1] **crook** dishonest person [2] **sole** only [3] **listless** having no energy

Students line up for school meals, made with locally produced foods, at Bar Sauri Primary School

and they couldn't afford to contribute food. So Mrs. Omolo and the 10 teachers paid for it themselves. [...]

The result was instantaneous[4]. Attendance among older children shot up to 100 percent, and their test scores followed suit[5]. Sauri went from 68th out of 353 schools in the district in 2000 to 7th in 2004.

"This year," Mrs. Omolo says, "we will be No. 1."

Part of the reason for her confidence is that this year, every schoolchild will eat. Sauri was chosen last year to be one of the United Nations' test villages – Koraro, Ethiopia, is the other – to show how poverty in Africa can be ended through programs that help villages directly. For the next five years, Sauri will receive dollar 250,000 a year for agricultural, educational and health programs. [...]

The United Nations plan, led by the economist Jeffrey D. Sachs, seeks to expand the program to the entire district, and then all over Africa. But that will happen only if the rich countries make good on their promise to ratchet up[6] foreign aid to 0.7 percent of G.D.P. by 2015. Britain, France and Germany have all put out timetables for meeting the goal. The United States, the world's richest country, has yet to do so.

---

[4] **instantaneous** happening immediately [5] **to follow suit** to do the same [6] **to ratchet up** *hochfahren*

Activities

A way out of poverty

1. Describe the development of Sauri's primary school into one of the best schools in Kenya.
2. How do the United Nations try to end poverty in Africa?
3. What lessons does the Sauri example teach us?

Talking about alleviating poverty

4. What could be your contribution to alleviate poverty in the world? With your partner collect ideas and discuss their feasibility in class.
5. Imagine you are Jeffrey D. Sachs, a representative of the UN, and had to give a talk on how to end poverty. Prepare this talk with reference to the texts you have read.

World Peace in Peril – Terrorism

Terrorism is not a phenomenon of the 20th century. When- and wherever in the world social or ethnic groups were suppressed and the military superiority of the repressive power could not be overcome by conventional means, the groups concerned often resorted to unconventional means to compensate their handicap.

Whereas in the past terrorists used to be motivated by social-revolutionary and ethnic-nationalistic intentions and goals, in recent years terrorism has been religious-fundamentally inspired and marked by the use of the technical facilities which globalisation offers. In fact, terrorism has become a global phenomenon.

The radical network of al Qaeda under the leadership of Osama Bin Laden seems to have developed an effective global-scale organisation and represents a threat to the whole world. It has planned and carried out the terrorist attacks all over the world, of which the one on the World Trade Centre in New York (9/11/2001) was the most devastating. It is also supposed to have masterminded the Madrid terrorist attacks (2004) and the Underground bombings in London (2005).

Ever since the New York terrorist attack and the Bush Administration's declaration of War on Terrorism the same year, America has been involved in military activities against states that are supposed to shelter terrorists. They defeated the Taliban regime in Afghanistan, they ousted Saddam Hussein from power in Iraq. However, they have not succeeded in stamping out terrorism, rather the opposite. The Islamic resistance seems to be increasing in both countries and has cost the Americans over 3000 soldiers' lives, killed in action so far.

The wreckage of a commuter train at a Madrid station on March 11, 2004, the work of local jihadists

The Logic of Terror

Niall Ferguson

▼ Concentrate on Osama bin Laden's motives.

Why did Osama bin Laden, himself a Saudi, order twenty-one of his followers, most of them also Saudis, to hijack four planes and fly them into the World Trade Center, the Pentagon and (in all likelihood) the White House?

In their Declaration of the World Islamic Front for Jihad Against the Jews and the Crusaders of February 23, 1998, he and his cosignatories[1] gave three reasons for issuing their notorious[2] fatwa[3] "to kill the Americans and their allies":

First, for over seven years the United States has been occupying the lands of Islam in the holiest places, the Arab Peninsula, plundering[4] its riches, dictating to its rulers, humiliating[5] its people, terrorizing its neighbours, and turning its bases in the Peninsula into a spearhead[6] through which to fight the neighboring Muslim peoples. [...]
Second, despite the great devastation[7] inflicted[8] on the Iraqi people by the crusader-Zionist alliance [...] the Americans are once again trying to repeat the horrific massacres [...]
Third, if the Americans' aims behind these wars are religious and economic, the aim is also to serve the Jews' petty state and divert[10] attention from its occupation of Jerusalem and murder of Muslims there. The best proof of this is their eagerness[11] to destroy Iraq, the strongest neighboring Arab state, and their endeavour[12] to fragment all the states of the region such as Iraq, Saudi Arabia, Egypt, and Sudan into paper statelets and through their disunion and weakness to guarantee Israel's survival and the continuation of the brutal crusade occupation of the Peninsula.

Study closely ▼ Ferguson's explanations.

The aim of killing Americans was therefore clear: it was in order "to liberate the al-Aqsa Mosque and the holy mosque [Mecca] from their grip[13], and in order for their armies to move out of all the lands of Islam, defeated and unable to threaten any Muslim." Bin Laden echoed these words in his interview published in *Time* magazine eleven months later and just eight months before the 9/11 attacks. His goal, in short, were to get the American forces out of Saudi Arabia, to get them out of the Middle East altogether, to overthrow Arab government sympathetic to the United States and to destroy the state of Israel. Subsequent statements attributed to him are consistent[14] on these points. Some Western commentators are deceived[15] by bin Laden's rhetoric of pan-Islamic, global jihad into imagining that he is a genuine harbinger[16] of a clash of civilizations. It would be more accurate to say that bin Laden is the offspring[17] of the Middle East's distinctive civilization of clashes, a retarded[18] political culture in which terrorism has long been a substitute for both peaceful politics and conventional warfare. No doubt it is gratifying[19] to imagine a collective Muslim sense of historical disenchantment[20], an old superiority complex that centuries of historic decline have transformed

The New Iraq – a civilisation of clashes

[1] **cosignatories** people who also sign document [2] **notorious** well-known for being bad
[3] **fatwa** official order made by an Islamic religious leader [4] **to plunder** to steal
[5] **to humiliate** to make sb. feel ashamed or stupid [6] **spearhead** leading group
[7] **devastation** destruction [8] **inflicted** having caused [9] **petty** small and unimportant
[10] **to divert** to distract [11] **eagerness** enthusiasm, excitement [12] **endeavour** striving
[13] **grip** firm hold [14] **consistent** behaving in the same way [15] **to deceive** to make sb. believe sth. [16] **harbinger** *Vorbote* [17] **offspring** child [18] **retarded** less developed
[19] **gratifying** pleasing and giving satisfaction [20] **disenchantment** disillusionment

into "a downward spiral of hate and spite[21], rage and self-pity, poverty and oppression." Yet the ideology of al Qaeda has relatively little in common with the belief system of the majority of people in the largest Muslim countries such as Indonesia and Turkey, to say nothing of the immigrant Muslim communities of the West. Even bin Laden's religious beliefs bear the idiosyncratic[22] hallmarks[23] of Wahhabism[24], which scarcely exists outside the desert of Arabia.

[21] **spite** nastiness [22] **idiosyncratic** eccentric, typical [23] **hallmark** distinctive feature
[24] **Wahhabism** branch of Islam reform movement that proclaims the simplicity of the early religion founded on the Koran and Sunna; influence is strong in Saudi Arabia

Activities

1. Summarise Osama bin Laden's motives and goals.
2. Ferguson offers explanations for the terrorist activities of Osama bin Laden and al Qaeda. What are they?
3. What do you think of his explanations?
4. Use the Internet or other publications for more background information about Osama bin Laden and al Qaeda and prepare a short talk.

bin Laden's motives and goals

Research on the Internet

The Best Ways to Beat Terror

Fareed Zakaria

▼ Pay special attention to Zakaria's explanation of terrorism and the countermeasures he suggests.

Last week the British Government foiled[1] what it believed was the largest terrorist plot ever in that country. Police arrested eight men, and seized[2] half a ton of ammonium nitrate, enough for an explosive five times as powerful as the Bali bombs that killed 200 people. The most striking aspect of the episode, however, is that the authorities see no involvement by Al Qaeda. In fact, not one of the suspects is foreign-born or had spent any time in the Afghan training camps. These are British middle-class Muslim suburbanites[3] who the authorities say became terrorists.

Most terror attacks over the past two years have been planned by groups like this one. They are inspired, not directed, by Al Qaeda, and draw their support from a variety of mostly private sources. Tackling the threat they pose[4] is the key to security in this age.

Terrorism today doesn't need government backing because it is fuelled by three broad forces: the openness of free societies, the easy access to technologies of violence and a radical, global ideology of hatred. It can be stopped only by responses at each level.

Fareed Zakaria

[1] **to foil** to stop sth. from happening [2] **to seize** to take sth. suddenly using force
[3] **suburbanite** person living in suburb [4] **to pose** to present

London attack, 2005

Western societies – increasingly others as well – provide enormous freedoms to people living within them. Terrorists use these freedoms to hide. Now we have to find them. This means, as Tony Blair said last week, measures such as national identity cards and biometric identification systems. It also means much deeper cooperation between law-enforcement[5] and intelligence agencies. People with known connections to terrorists should be picked up, at least for detailed questioning, if not detention[6]. We need pre-emption[7], but of individuals more than of states.
Explosives that used to be difficult to obtain are now a phone call away. Esoteric know-how is posted on Web sites. We can't fight the dispersion of knowledge, but we can stop the dispersion[8] of deadly materials. The errors over Iraq should not obscure[9] the reality that terrorists are seeking chemical, biological and nuclear weapons, and would not hesitate to use them. Counter-proliferation[10] – using bribes[11], sanctions and even, on occasion, military force – needs to move to the center of foreign policy.
What drives terrorism, however, is not easy means but strong motives. Militant, political Islam has brainwashed thousands of young Muslims around the world who believe it is their duty to fight against the modern world. This ideology of hatred has grown as the Western-supported "moderate" regimes of die Middle East miserably failed to deliver[12] economic opportunity or political freedom to their people. [...]
That's why the only way to combat this new global terror is to fight the ideology that fires it everywhere. So the war on terror is really a war of ideas. And I'm not sure we are winning it.

---

[5] **law-enforcement** police force [6] **detention** imprisonment [7] **pre-emption** action to prevent sth. from happening [8] **dispersion** spreading out [9] **to obscure** to cover up [10] **counter-proliferation** action that prevents the increase in number [11] **bribe** *Bestechung* [12] **to deliver** to produce

Activities

Fighting terrorism

1. What does the British example show?
2. Fareed Zakaria describes the forces that fuel terrorism and suggests countermeasures. Explain.

Your point of view

3. What do you think of Fareed Zakaria's ideas?
4. Fareed Zakaria uses the expression "a war of ideas". What does he mean by it? Do you agree or disagree with him as to his final conclusion?
5. Taking everything you have learnt about terrorism into account write a short essay on the topic "The best ways to beat terror as a global threat".

International Peace-Keeping: The Role of the USA and the UN

The Second World War ended with the **United States** and the Soviet Union being the only superpowers in the world. The confrontation that ensued between the two (Cold War) lasted for 45 years and ended with the collapse of the Soviet Union. A major conflict between the two superpowers was prevented by the doctrine of MAD (mutually assured destruction – *Gleichgewicht des Schreckens*). In the Post-Cold-War world America established itself as the most powerful nation in the world, militarily as well as economically, politically and culturally. And whenever its commercial interests or its commitment to freedom and democracy were at stake it applied its power relentlessly. Its unilateral actions, in particular its intervention in Iraq with a coalition of the willing, have been interpreted as a rejection of the multilateral approach that is typical of twenty-first-century global politics. Critics of America's unilateral approach in dealing with global problems expect America to assume a global role again as a key player in the interest of strong global institutions and global peace and security. It remains to be seen whether in the Post-Post-Cold-War period, which has witnessed the emergence of China and India, and the resurrection of the Soviet Union as global players, America will be forced to adopt a more responsible and less selfish attitude and use its power and resources not only unilaterally in its own interest. The world cannot do without America, it needs America in a peace-keeping role, and yet it is up to America to realise that it cannot do without the rest of the world, either.

The **United Nations** were founded after the Second World War by 51 states with three major goals in mind: to maintain international peace and security, to develop friendly relations among nations and to promote the cooperation among nations in solving international, social, cultural and humanitarian problems. As an institution it has played and is still playing a key role in the development of present-day globalisation.

During the period of the Cold War its peace-keeping function was overshadowed by the two superpowers – the SU and the USA. Since then, i.e. the beginning of the 1990s, it has played an active peace-keeping role in the First Gulf War, in the conflicts in former Yugoslavia and in several African states (Angola, Mozambique, Sierra Leona, Somalia, Sudan-Darfur). The role of the UN as a global supranational political institution has not gone unchallenged, the Bush administration has particularly tried to undermine and diminish its authority. It remains to be seen if it can regain the peace-keeping role it played during the 1990s.

Remarks at the United Nations General Assembly

George W. Bush

When on the 12th of September 2002 the United Nations General Assembly discussed the Iraq crisis President Bush tried to urge the delegates of the different countries to support a resolution in favour of intervention. He particularly referred to Saddam Hussein as a danger to peace and stability in the world. He pointed out that Saddam Hussein had broken all the commitments he had accepted after the First Gulf War (1991) and that he had not been prepared to give UN inspectors unrestricted access to verify Iraq's obligation to get rid of weapons of mass destruction and long-range missiles.

While reading ▼ underline Bush's accusations and demands.

[...] As we meet today, it's been almost four years since the last UN inspectors set foot in Iraq, four years for the Iraqi regime to plan, and to build, and to test behind the cloak[1] of secrecy.

We know that Saddam Hussein pursued[2] weapons of mass murder even when inspectors were in his country. Are we to assume that he stopped when they left? The history, the logic, and the facts lead to one conclusion: Saddam Hussein's regime is a grave[3] and gathering[4] danger. To suggest otherwise is to hope against the evidence. To assume this regime's good faith is to bet the lives of millions and the peace of the world in a reckless[5] gamble. And this is a risk we must not take.

Delegates to the General Assembly, we have been more than patient. We've tried sanctions. We've tried the carrot of oil for food, and the stick of coalition military strikes. But Saddam Hussein has defied[6] all these efforts and continues to develop weapons of mass destruction. The first time we may be completely certain he has nuclear weapons is when, God forbids, he uses one. We owe it to all our citizens to do everything in our power to prevent that day from coming.

The conduct of the Iraqi regime is a threat to the authority of the United Nations, and a threat to peace. Iraq has answered a decade of UN demands with a decade of defiance[7]. All the world now faces a test, and the United Nations a difficult and defining moment. Are Security Council resolutions to be honored and enforced, or cast aside without consequence? Will the United Nations serve the purpose of its founding, or will it be irrelevant?

The United States helped found the United Nations. We want the United Nations to be effective, and respectful, and successful. We want the resolutions of the world's most important multilateral body to be enforced. And right now those resolutions are being unilaterally subverted[8] by the

---

[1] **cloak** cover [2] **to pursue** to strive for [3] **grave** very serious [4] **to gather** to increase [5] **reckless** irresponsible [6] **to defy** to disobey [7] **defiance** disobedience [8] **to subvert** to undermine

Iraqi regime. Our partnership of nations can meet the test before us, by making clear what we now expect of the Iraqi regime.
If the Iraqi regime wishes peace, it will immediately and unconditionally forswear[9], disclose, and remove or destroy all weapons of mass destruction, long-range missiles, and all related material.
If the Iraqi regime wishes peace, it will immediately end all support for terrorism and act to suppress it, as all states are required to do by UN Security Council resolutions.
If the Iraqi regime wishes peace, it will cease[10] persecution[11] of its civilian population, including Shi'a, Sunnis, Kurds, Turkomans, and others, again as required by Security Council resolutions.
If the Iraqi regime wishes peace, it will release or account for all Gulf War personnel whose fate is still unknown. It will return the remains of any who are deceased[12], return stolen property, accept liability[13] for losses resulting from the invasion of Kuwait, and fully cooperate with international efforts to resolve these issues, as required by Security Council resolutions.
If the Iraqi regime wishes peace, it will immediately end all illicit[14] trade outside the oil-for-food program. It will accept UN administration of funds from that program, to ensure that the money is used fairly and promptly for the benefit of the Iraqi people.
If all these steps are taken, it will signal a new openness and accountability[15] in Iraq. And it could open the prospect of the United Nations helping to build a government that represents all Iraqis – a government based on respect for human rights, economic liberty, and internationally supervised elections.
The United States has no quarrel with the Iraqi people; they've suffered too long in silent captivity. Liberty for the Iraqi people is a great moral cause, and a great strategic goal. The people of Iraq deserve it; the security of all nations requires it. Free societies do not intimidate[16] through cruelty and conquest[17], and open societies do not threaten the world with mass murder. The United States supports political and economic liberty in a unified Iraq.
We can harbor[18] no illusions – and that's important today to remember. Saddam Hussein attacked Iran in 1980 and Kuwait in 1990. He's fired ballistic missiles at Iran and Saudi Arabia, Bahrain, and Israel. His regime once ordered the killing of every person between the ages of 15 and 70 in certain Kurdish villages in northern Iraq. He has gassed many Iranians, and 40 Iraqi villages.
My nation will work with the UN Security Council to meet our common challenge. If Iraq's regime defies us again, the world must move deliberately, decisively to hold Iraq to account[19]. We will work with the UN Security Council for the necessary resolutions. But the purposes of the United States should not be doubted. The Security Council resolutions will be enforced – the just demands of peace and security will be met – or action will be unavoidable. And a regime that has lost its legitimacy will also lose its power.
Events can turn in one of two ways: If we fail to act in the face of danger, the people of Iraq will continue to live in brutal submission[20]. The regime will

---

[9] **to forswear** to give up [10] **to cease** to end [11] **persecution** oppression [12] **deceased** dead [13] **liability** legal responsibility [14] **illicit** illegal [15] **accountability** responsibility [16] **to intimidate** to frighten or threaten [17] **conquest** act of getting control of [18] **to harbor** to keep in mind [19] **to hold to account** to make responsible for [20] **submission** capitulation

Collateral damage

have new power to bully[21] and dominate and conquer its neighbors, condemning the Middle East to more years of bloodshet[22] and fear. The regime will remain unstable – the region will remain unstable, with little hope of freedom, and isolated from the progress of our times. With every step the Iraqi regime takes toward gaining and deploying[23] the most terrible weapons, our own options to confront that regime will narrow. And if an emboldened[24] regime were to supply these weapons to terrorist allies, then the attacks of September the 11th would be a prelude to far greater horrors.

If we meet our responsibilities, if we overcome this danger, we can arrive at a very different future. The people of Iraq can shake off their captivity[25]. They can one day join a democratic Afghanistan and a democratic Palestine, inspiring reforms throughout the Muslim world. These nations can show by their example that honest government, and respect for women, and the great Islamic tradition of learning can triumph in the Middle East and beyond. And we will show that the promise of the United Nations can be fulfilled in our time.

Neither of these outcomes is certain. Both have been set before us. We must choose between a world of fear and a world of progress. We cannot stand by and do nothing while dangers gather. We must stand up for our security, and for the permanent rights and the hopes of mankind. By heritage and by choice, the United States of America will make that stand. And, delegates to the United Nations, you have the power to make that stand, as well.

Thank you very much. (Applause)

---

[21] **to bully** to make sb. do sth. using force or threats [22] **bloodshed** *Blutvergießen*
[23] **to deploy** to organise troops so that they are ready for action [24] **emboldened** encouraged [25] **captivity** state of being imprisoned

Activities

Bush, the Iraq, the UN and the world

1. What does Bush accuse Iraq of?
2. Make a list of Bush's demands on the Iraq.
3. What does his speech reveal about his attitude towards the UN and about America's role in the globalised world?

The speaker's strategies

4. Point out the strategies Bush uses to convince the delegates.

Your opinion

5. What do you think of his speech? Discuss your opinion with your neighbour and then write a critical comment.
6. An American reporter recently wrote in a newspaper article that American politics suffer from a discrepancy between high-minded idealism and low practice. Can this statement be applied in this context? Explain.

New World Order – Remaking the United Nations

Reactions to the position of the Bush administration were produced even before the vote on the resolution was taken by the United Nations General Assembly. For the writer of this comment, cooperative internationalism rather than unilateral action is the answer to the challenges of our times.

▼ Try to understand what the author means by "new world order".

As matters stand, the result of the security council's forthcoming[1] vote on Iraq will almost certainly be rejected by the "losing" side. From this likely failure to attain[2] consensus on a matter as significant as the invasion and occupation of an independent, sovereign state, far-reaching consequences may flow for the UN itself. If the US and Britain are unable to win majority support, and even if the resolution is vetoed, they are expected to go to war regardless. If the resolution is carried, opponents will still justly maintain[3] that it does not explicitly authorise force, contravenes[4] international law, is driven by political considerations, and is partly attributable to US vote-buying. This is no mere passing difference of opinion. It could mark a potentially fatal rupture to the UN's founding principles.

Both sides claim to act in the UN's best interests. US and British officials say the UN must act on Iraq now or be rendered[5] irrelevant, perhaps permanently. This argument ignores the fact that the UN is already acting, principally through the inspections process. What they really mean is that if the UN does not deliver the outcome they want, they will ignore it. George Bush's clear message is that if and when such disputes arise in future, the US might bypass the UN altogether.

In their corner, French and German officials argue the opposite – that the UN will only remain relevant and effective if the previously agreed Iraq policy of coercive[6] disarmament and, more broadly, traditional security council procedural[7] and legal norms are upheld. This is entirely reasonable, up to a point. But what they and other opponents fail to address, at least in public, is the more fundamental dilemma of how best to co-opt[8] or contain one UN member – the US – that is uniquely and disproportionately powerful; how best to work with the US instead of being steamrollered by it. This problem has been brewing ever since the US emerged as sole superpower. But it has taken a rogue[9] US administration

The world order according to Bush

---

[1] **forthcoming** planned [2] **to attain** to obtain [3] **to maintain** to claim, to believe [4] **to contravene** to break [5] **to render** to become [6] **coercive** forced [7] **procedural** *verfahrenstechnisch* [8] **to co-opt** to integrate [9] **rogue** *Schurke*

ideologically antipathetic to multilateral restraints[10] as typified by the UN and by international treaties to bring the problem to a head. In this wider context, Iraq is but a harbinger[11] of things to come. For this reason, it is a watershed[12] event.

Some common sense, common ground reminders are needed at this point. If the UN did not exist, it would have to be invented; a globalised society requires a primary global forum to oversee its affairs. But the UN is the sum of its parts. If it falls, it does so because its controlling national components fall. To say, with Mr Bush, that the US can act without the UN in Iraq is foolishness. UN agencies will have a crucial post-war role to play and sensible US policymakers recognise this fact. Only the UN can confer[13] international legitimacy on such a US policy. Without legitimacy and the active support of other nations, US hopes to implant democracy in Iraq and nurture[14] a wider regional reformation will founder[15].

In other words, the mutuality of interest upon which the UN has always rested still applies, possibly even more so now. Powerful though it is, the US must recollect[16] and embrace[17] this basic fact of interdependence that it once understood so well. Ironically, the sheer scale[18] of postwar problems may force it to do so. Other states, from Britain and France to developing country alliances, must meanwhile join in redressing[19] the imbalance of power through reform of security council membership along supranational or geographical lines and by pooling[20] sovereignty. Mr Bush may not get it – but he will not be president for ever. A renewed, imaginative commitment to cooperative internationalism is the only way ahead.

---

[10] **restraint** restriction [11] **harbinger** a sign that sth. is going to happen [12] **watershed** *Wasserscheide* [13] **to confer** to give officially [14] **to nurture** to raise [15] **to founder** to fail, to break down [16] **to recollect** to remember, to recall [17] **to embrace** to accept [18] **sheer scale** *das schiere Ausmaß* [19] **to redress** to remedy [20] **to pool** to combine

Activities

The old and the new world order

1. Summarise the writer's arguments.
2. Explain what he means by "new world order".

The writer's attitude

3. Analyse the writer's attitude to the position of the Bush administration.

Reactions to Bush's speech

4. What do you think of the writer's arguments? Which ones have turned out to be true?
5. Use the Internet to find out more about the reactions to the position of the Bush administration at the time.

The Future Role of America

Jim Garrison

ESTABLISHING EFFECTIVE GLOBAL GOVERNANCE[1] BEFORE THE DELUGE[2]

Today, again, what seems impossible is in fact imperative. The current crises are overwhelming[3], but they must be solved. The system of sovereign nation-states seems eternal but must be transformed. The world is crippled by ineffective government, but it can be delivered by network governance. The world community is critical of the United States, but it requires American leadership.

If the United States would affirm rather than oppose these kinds of measures, it would find the better part of the world ready to begin collaborating, just as both Wilson and Roosevelt[4] did. The world is weary[5] of conflict. It is ready for inspirational leadership and audacious[6] action. The international community is ready to eliminate[7] HIV/AIDS, it is ready to take action on global warming, it is ready to eliminate poverty. People are yearning[8] for somebody from somewhere to bring about a more equitable[9] and effective management of the global system.

For America to simply chase the shadows of terrorists and consolidate military hegemony in the face of the totality of our global challenges is to completely miss the point of world affairs in this first decade of the new millennium. If America would protect the world militarily while building cooperative structures, champion the free market while emphasizing the common good, and use its national sovereignty to pioneer network democracy at a global level, it could be not only the greatest empire the world has ever known but also the final empire. The world could be integrated by these actions to such an extent that it could evolve into a mosaic of interconnections and interdependencies in which empire would no longer be needed.

This is not to say that American power would be weakened. As Wilson, Roosevelt and Truman[10] demonstrated, working to enhance[11] the community of nations only enhances American prestige, influence, and respect. This is the point and paradox of stewardship[12].

In short, the opportunity before America and the world is this: the League of Nations was established in the ashes of the First World War, the United Nations in the ashes of the Second World War. The challenge now is for the United States to build on these achievements and lead in the building of the next iteration[13] of global governance.

But the United States and the world community must ensure that this time the next global governance regime is implemented proactively, before the catastrophe that will inevitably ensue[14] if our global challenges are not solved. Can the United States be so inspirational in its leadership of the world that it prevents the kind of catastrophe that produced the other two advances in

▼ Focus on the role the author envisages for the USA.

President Woodrow Wilson (1856–1924), when fighting for the League of Nations said, "I would rather fail in a cause that I know some day will triumph than to win in a cause that I know some day will fail."

---

1 **governance** control 2 **deluge** flood 3 **to overwhelm** to overpower 4 **Wilson** US president (1913–1921) from Democratic Party, established a new vision of America's role in the world **Roosevelt** US president (1933–1945) from Democratic Party, developed New Deal at the time of the Great Depression 5 **weary** very tired 6 **audacious** bold 7 **to eliminate** to get rid of 8 **to yearn for** to long for 9 **equitable** fair 10 **Truman** US president (1949–1953) from Republican Party, developed Truman Doctrine to check communist expansion 11 **to enhance** to improve 12 **stewardship** leadership 13 **iteration** repetition 14 **to ensue** to follow

The United Nations headquarters in New York City, completed in 1950

global governance? Can it prevent the repetition of the most ancient pattern in human history, that real change never actually comes until *after* a crisis? Can the human community break out of this chain of cause and effect?
The next catastrophe, whenever and wherever it arises, will, again, be global. We can be sure of that. It will affect, if not consume, us all. World War I and World War II were both global conflagrations[15]. They affected the whole world. This could happen again, only the next time with more virulence and destructive effect. [...]
American leadership at this time in history is crucial[16], provided that America combines its light with its power in such a way that the integrating institutions and mechanisms needed for the effective management of the global system are infused with the same kind of radical democracy with which America itself was founded. A global system of governance, based on inclusive democratic principles, would make impossible the emergence[17] of any other nation-state with imperial ambitions, for the planet will have united as a single matrix[18] of collaborative, self-regulating connections. America's great contribution to history, as the first global democratic empire, could be to make obsolete the necessity for empire.
The challenge to America is whether it can rise to the occasion and provide the kind of global leadership that will seize[19] the opportunities buried in our crises. Midwifing[20] a democratic global system, before going through a global cataclysm[21], will not be an easy task. If it succeeds, America will gain the accolade[22] of greatness. If it fails, America will be consigned[23] the opprobrium[24] of tragedy. [...]
Given what is at stake for its own people and for the whole world, may it make its choices guided by the wisdom of its past and with the intention of exercising its power in service of the light by which it was founded. What is at stake is nothing less than the foundations of the first planetary civilization.

---

[15] **conflagration** *Feuersbrunst* [16] **crucial** essential [17] **emergence** process of coming into existence [18] **matrix** framework [19] **to seize** to grab, to make use of [20] **to midwife** to help to come into existence [21] **cataclysm** catastrophe [22] **accolade** praise [23] **to consign** to hand to [24] **opprobrium** *Schmach*

Activities

The state of the world and the global role of the US

1. Analyse the author's description of the present state of the world affairs and the solutions he suggests.
2. What global role does the author envisage for the US in this situation?
3. What would be the consequences not only for the US if it accepted the envisaged role?

The author's techniques

4. Does the author sound convincing to you? Analyse the techniques he uses to convince you.

America's decision

5. In your opinion, will America rise to the occasion and thus make an important contribution to the peace and security in our globalised world or will it fail and simply consolidate its military power?

The Farewell Address

Kofi Annan

This newspaper article is based on a speech Kofi Annan was scheduled to deliver on December 11, 2006, at the Harry S. Truman Presidential Library in Independence, Missouri. In this final speech as Secretary-General, he referred to the founding of the United Nations emphasising the necessity for the United States to return to President Truman's multilateralist foreign policies.

▼ Find out about Kofi Annan's indirect criticism of the USA and about the role he envisages for the UN.

WASHINGTON – Nearly 50 years ago, when I arrived in Minnesota as a student fresh from Africa, I had much to learn – starting with the fact that there is nothing wimpish[1] about wearing earmuffs[2] when it is 15 degrees below zero. All my life since has been a learning experience. Now I want to pass on five lessons I have learned during 10 years as secretary-general of the United Nations that I believe the community of nations needs to learn as it confronts the challenges of the 21st century.

1. First, in today's world we are all responsible for each other's security. Against such threats as nuclear proliferation[3], climate change, global pandemics[4] or terrorists operating from safe havens[5] in failed states, no nation can make itself secure by seeking supremacy[6] over all others. Only by working to make each other secure can we hope to achieve lasting security for ourselves. This responsibility includes our shared responsibility to protect people from genocide, war crimes, ethnic cleansing[7] and crimes against humanity. That was accepted by all nations at last year's UN summit. But when we look at the murder, rape[8] and starvation[9] still being inflicted[10] on the people of Darfur, we realize that such doctrines remain pure rhetoric unless those with the power to intervene effectively – by exerting political, economic or, in the last resort, military muscle – are prepared to take the lead. It also includes a responsibility to future generations to preserve resources[11] that belong to them as well as to us. Every day that we do nothing, or too little, to prevent climate change imposes[12] higher costs on our children.

2. Second, we are also responsible for each other's welfare. Without a measure of solidarity, no society can be truly stable. It is not realistic to think that some people can go on deriving great benefits[13] from globalisation while billions of others are left in, or thrown into, abject[14] poverty. We have to give all human beings at least a chance to share in our prosperity.

3. Third, both security and prosperity depend on respect for human rights and the rule of law. Throughout history human life has been enriched by diversity, and different communities have learned from each other. But if our communities are to live in peace we must stress also what unites us:

---

[1] **wimpish** weak and afraid [2] **earmuffs** *Ohrenschützer* [3] **proliferation** rapid increase in number [4] **pandemics** *Seuche* [5] **haven** shelter, refuge [6] **supremacy** dominance [7] **ethnic cleansing** *ethnische Säuberung* [8] **rape** the act of violently forcing a woman to have sex [9] **starvation** suffering caused by lack of food [10] **to inflict on** to make sb. suffer, to impose [11] **resource** sth. such as useful land, minerals, oil, etc. [12] **to impose** to force sb. to accept sth. [13] **benefit** advantage [14] **abject** shameful and depressing

our common humanity and the need for our human dignity and rights to be protected by law.
That is vital for development, too. Both foreigners and a country's own citizens are more likely to invest when their basic rights are protected and they know they will be fairly treated under the law. Policies that genuinely favor development are more likely to be adopted if the people most in need of development can make their voice heard. States need to play by the rules toward each other, as well. No community suffers from too much rule of law, many suffer from too little – and the international community is among them.

4. My fourth lesson therefore is that governments must be accountable[15] for their actions, in the international as well as the domestic arena. Every state owes some account to other states on which its actions have a decisive impact[16]. As things stand, poor and weak states are easily held to account, because they need foreign aid. But large and powerful states, whose actions have the greatest impact on others, can be constrained[17] only by their own people.
That gives the people and institutions of powerful states a special responsibility to take account of global views and interests. And today they need to take into account also what we call "non-state actors." States can no longer – if they ever could – confront global challenges alone. Increasingly, they need help from the myriad[18] types of association in which people come together voluntarily, to profit or to think about, and change, the world.

[15] **accountable** answerable [16] **impact** great effect [17] **to constrain** to restrict [18] **myriad** large number

5. How can states hold each other to account? Only through multilateral institutions. So my final lesson is that those institutions must be organized in a fair and democratic way, giving the poor and the weak some influence over the actions of the rich and the strong.

Developing countries should have a stronger voice in international financial institutions, whose decisions can mean life or death for their people. New permanent or long-term members should be added to the UN Security Council, whose current membership reflects the reality of 1945, not of today.

No less important, all the Security Council's members must accept the responsibility that comes with their privilege. The council is not a stage for acting out national interests. It is the management committee of our fledgling[19] global security system.

More than ever, Americans, like the rest of humanity, need a functioning global system. Experience has shown, time and again, that the system works poorly when the United States remains aloof[20] but it functions much better when there is farsighted U.S. leadership.

That gives American leaders of today and tomorrow a great responsibility. The American people must see that they live up to it.

---

[19] **fledgling** inexperienced [20] **aloof** distant, detached

Activities

Kofi Annan's legacy

1. Make notes of what you regard as the gist of Kofi Annan's 5 lessons. Compare your notes with those of your neighbour and discuss points of agreement and disagreement.
2. How – according to Kofi Annan – can peace and security be achieved in a globalised world? What role does he envisage for the UN in this context?
3. Point out the direct and indirect criticisms levelled at the policies of the United States.
4. In a few sentences explain the writer's line of argumentation.

Peace put up for discussion

5. What is your opinion of Kofi Annan's ideas?
6. Compare Kofi Annan's ideas about peace and security with those conveyed in the other texts of this unit. Point out similarities and differences.
7. Prepare a formal debate about the following thesis: "To secure peace in the world this house would rather support unilateralist action than not do anything at all".

The Human Faces Behind Globalisation

Just imagine what the world was like before the age of globalisation: nations, countries, regions neatly set apart and divided by natural or political borders. Closer ties in the form of mutual interaction only occurred where some common interest such as trade relations, political projects (tragically enough often as military interventions and wars), cultural ties or religious missions were at stake.

The great migrations in the history of mankind and very often as a consequence of wars and natural catastrophes gradually, – and we are talking about centuries now –, changed the monolithic structure of a world society. Scientific progress and technological advancement have helped to create an infrastructure that links even the remotest parts of the world within hours or days and, digitally speaking, even in fragments of seconds. In human terms so to speak, the effect of globalisation is the global village where many ethnicities, cultures and faiths live side by side. This section of the book tries to present the effects of cultural interchange and exposure to different cultures on people.

Activity

Different biographies

Look at the picture. Can you trace where the different people come from? What do you know about their place of origin, their culture, their faith? Draw up an imaginary biography which you can compare later with the information supplied in the texts to follow.

Western Literature as an Eye-Opener

Dai Sijie

Globalisation and information are closely linked, indeed they are interdependent. That is why the media play such an important role. The printed and the audio-visual media, above all film and television, available all around the globe, have helped us to get in touch with foreign countries and cultures. Few countries, however, have this free flow of ideas. The Internet though has broken these last obstacles. In the history of many nations you find examples of a self-imposed or enforced isolation – and also ways to avoid it and act against it even at the risk of severe punishment.
This is shown in Dai Sijie's novel, *Balzac and the Little Chinese Seamstress*. It is during the 1971 Cultural Revolution in China under Mao that two boys, both sons of doctors and thus members of the privileged class, are sent to a re-education camp where they find a hidden treasure – Western novels.

▼ Find out what role literature plays in the lives of the two boys.

It was all such a long time ago, but one particular image from our stint of re-education is still etched[1] in my memory with extraordinary precision: a red-beaked raven keeping watch as Luo[2] crawled along a narrow track with a yawning chasm[3] on either side. On his back he carried the inconspicuous[4], work-soiled[5] bamboo hod[6] in which he had secreted *Old Go*, as Balzac's *Père Goriot* was titled in Chinese – the book he was going to read to the Little Seamstress, the lovely mountain girl in need of culture.
During the whole month of September following our successful burglary we were seduced[7], overwhelmed[8], spellbound[9] by the mystery of the outside world, especially the world of women, love and sex as revealed to us by these Western writers day after day, page after page, book after book. Not only had Four-Eyes[10] left the mountain without daring to denounce[11] us, also, as luck would have it, our headman had gone away to the town of Yong Jing to attend a Communist Party conference. In the ensuing[12] political vacuum our village lapsed[13] into quiet anarchy, and Luo and I stopped going to work in the fields without the villagers – themselves unwilling converts[14] from opium farmers to guardians of our souls – raising the slightest objection[15]. I kept my door more securely locked than ever and passed the time with foreign novels. Since Balzac was Luo's favourite I put him to one side, and with the ardour and earnestness of my eighteen years I fell in love with one author after another: Flaubert, Gogol, Melville, and even Romain Rolland.
Let me tell you about Romain Rolland. Among the books in Four-Eyes's suitcase there was only one by him: volume one of his four-volume master-

---

[1] **to etch** to imprint, to engrave [2] **Luo** the first-person-narrator's boyhood friend [3] **chasm** deep abyss [4] **inconspicuous** not easy to spot [5] **work-soiled** showing signs of having been used [6] **hod** wooden box attached to a pole [7] **to seduce** to attract, to win over [8] **to overwhelm** to overpower the senses [9] **spellbound** magically attracted [10] **Four Eyes** (*infml.*) person wearing glasses [11] **to denounce** to condemn openly [12] **to ensue** to follow [13] **to lapse into** to fall into [14] **convert** sb. who has changed his faith and his life [15] **objection** argument or reason against sth.

China under Chairman Mao: A tell-tale picture

piece, *Jean-Christophe*. The Chinese translation was by Fu Lei, who also did the Balzac translations. As the story was about a musician and I myself played pieces on the violin such as *Mozart is Thinking of Chairman Mao*, I was naturally drawn to the book. I had intended only a brief flirtation[16], a skim[17] read, but once I had opened the book I couldn't put it down. Until then short stories had been my favourite reading: well wrought and sparkling with ideas, tales that made you laugh or took your breath away, that would stay with you for the rest of your days. I was more dubious about full-length novels. But Jean-Christophe, with his fierce individualism utterly untainted[18] by malice[19], was a salutary[20] revelation[21]. Without him I would never have understood the splendour of taking free and independent action as an individual. Up until this stolen encounter[22] with Romain Rolland's hero, my poor educated and re-educated brains had been incapable of grasping the notion of one man standing up against the whole world. The flirtation turned into a grand passion. Even the excessively emphatic style occasionally indulged in by the author did not detract from the beauty of this astonishing work of art. I was carried away, swept along by the mighty stream of words pouring from the hundreds of pages. To me it was the ultimate book: once you had read it, neither your own life nor the world you lived in would ever look the same.

---

[16] **flirtation** coquetry [17] **skim** first glance [18] **untainted** not spoiled, immaculate [19] **malice** evil intent [20] **salutary** intended to improve [21] **revelation** making known what was secret [22] **encounter** meeting, coming together

Activities

Living under Mao

1. Explain the situation the boys are in.

The hidden treasures

2. What makes the discovery and burglary of forbidden Western literature so extraordinary for the boys?
3. What strategies does the author use to influence the reader?

The importance of literature

4. Has a foreign literary work had a similar effect on you? Explain why.

Among the most immediate effects of globalisation dealt with in literary works are the identity crisis of the heroes and the constant conflict between their native culture and the new culture with its different values and norms, as well as different ways of life and customs. Between the extreme poles of assimilating to the host culture and rejecting one's native identity on the one hand, and keeping apart from the new country and living in a parallel society on the other hand, there are many forms of coping with the new life and a confused identity.
The following excerpts, the first one from the novel *The Namesake*, the second from the short story *The Third and Final Continent* are by the same author, Jhumpa Lahiri.

Confused Identity

Jhumpa Lahiri

In the novel *The Namesake* Jhumpa Lahiri writes about the identity conflict of a young American born to Indian immigrants in the United States. As is the custom in India, the name-giving of the new-born child is the grandparents' duty. But because the letter from India has obviously been lost on its way to the New World the boy's father gives him the name of Gogol, his favourite Russian writer. Much later, when at university, he takes on a new name, Nikhil, which, however, does not reflect his longed for American identity any more than Gogol did.

▼ Pay attention to how Gogol feels and behaves at the panel discussion.

One day he attends a panel discussion about Indian novels written in English. He feels obligated to attend; one of the presenters on the panel[1], Amit, is a distant cousin who lives in Bombay, whom Gogol has never met. His mother has asked him to greet Amit on her behalf. Gogol is bored by the panelists, who keep referring to something called "marginality[2]," as if it were some sort of medical condition. For most of the hour, he sketches portraits of the panelists, who sit hunched[3] over their papers along a rectangular table. "Teleologically[4] speaking, ABCDs are unable to answer the question 'Where are you from?'" the sociologist on the panel declares. Gogol has never heard the term *ABCD*. He eventually gathers that it stands for "American-born confused deshi." In other words, him. He learns that the *C* could also stand for "conflicted." He knows that *deshi*, a generic[5] word for "countryman," means "Indian," knows that his parents and all their friends always refer to India simply as *desh*. But Gogol never thinks of India as desh. He thinks of it as Americans do, as India.
Gogol slouches[6] in his seat and ponders[7] certain awkward truths. For instance, although he can understand his mother tongue, and speak it fluently, he cannot read or write it with even modest proficieny[8]. On trips to India his American-accented English is a source of endless amusement to his relatives, and when he and Sonia[9] speak to each other, aunts and uncles and cousins always shake their heads in disbelief and say, "I didn't understand a

---

[1] **panel** group of people to discuss a topic before an audience [2] **marginality** not belonging to the centre [3] **hunched** bowed [4] **teleological** believing in a purpose and design [5] **generic** referring to a group or class [6] **to slouch** to sit casually [7] **to ponder** to reflect on, to meditate [8] **proficiency** competence [9] **Sonia** Gogol's younger sister

word!" Living with a pet name[10] and a good name, in a place where such distinctions do not exist – surely that was emblematic[11] of the greatest confusion of all. He searches the audience for someone he knows, but it isn't his crowd – lots of lit majors with leather satchels and gold-rimmed glasses and fountain pens, lots of people Ruth[12] would have waved to. There are also lots of ABCDs. He has no idea there are this many on campus. He has no ABCD friends at college. He avoids them, for they remind him too much of the way his parents choose to live, befriending people not so much because they like them, but because of a past they happen to share. "Gogol, why aren't you a member of the Indian association here?" Amit asks later when they go for a drink at the Anchor. "I just don't have the time," Gogol says, not telling his well-meaning cousin that he can think of no greater hypocrisy[13] than joining an organization that willingly celebrates occasions his parents forced him, throughout his childhood and adolescence, to attend. "I'm Nikhil now," Gogol says, suddenly depressed by how many more times he will have to say this, asking people to remember, reminding them to forget, feeling as if an errata[14] slip were perpetually[15] pinned to his chest.

[10] **pet name** (as opposed to good name) Indian custom of differing between a name used by the family and a name for official purposes [11] **emblematic** here: typical [12] **Ruth** Gogol's liberal New York middle-class girl friend [13] **hypocrisy** *Heuchelei* [14] **errata** (*lat.*) printing errors [15] **perpetual** for all time, eternal

The Achievement Beyond Imagination

Jhumpa Lahiri

In the short story with the revealing title of *The Third and Final Continent* (after native India and the transitory destination of England, the final destination of Boston) we meet the parents and their son who have both settled down in the New World.

Find out why the ▼ parents want their son to stick to their native customs.

As for me, I have not strayed[1] much farther. Mala and I live in a town about twenty miles from Boston, on a tree-lined street much like Mrs. Croft's, in a house we own, with a garden that saves us from buying tomatoes in summer, and room for guests. We are American citizens now, so that we can collect social security[2] when it is time. Though we visit Calcutta every few years, and bring back more drawstring pajamas and Darjeeling tea, we have decided to grow old here. I work in a small college library. We have a son who attends Harvard University. Mala no longer drapes[3] the end of her sari over her head, or weeps at night for her parents, but occasionally she weeps for our son. So we drive to Cambridge to visit him, or bring him home for a weekend, so that he can eat rice with us with his hands, and speak in Bengali, things we sometimes worry he will no longer do after we die.
Whenever we make that drive, I always make it a point to take Massachusetts Avenue, in spite of the traffic. I barely recognize the buildings now, but each

[1] **to stray** to wander, to move on [2] **to collect social security** to claim money after one has retired [3] **to drape** to hang round, to cover with

time I am there I return instantly to those six weeks as if they were only the other day, and I slow down and point to Mrs. Croft's street, saying to my son, here was my first home in America, where I lived with a woman who was 103. "Remember?", Mala says, and smiles, amazed, as I am, that there was ever a time that we were strangers. My son always expresses his astonishment, not at Mrs. Croft's age, but at how little I paid in rent, a fact nearly as inconceivable[4] to him as a flag on the moon was to a woman born in 1866. In my son's eyes I see the ambition that had first hurled[5] me across the world. In a few years he will graduate and pave his way, alone and unprotected. But I remind myself that he has a father who is still living, a mother who is happy and strong. Whenever he is discouraged, I tell him that if I can survive on three continents, then there is no obstacle he cannot conquer. While the astronauts, heroes forever, spent mere hours on the moon, I have remained in this new world for nearly thirty years. I know that my achievement is quite ordinary. I am not the only man to seek his fortune far from home, and certainly I am not the first. Still, there are times I am bewildered by each mile I have traveled, each meal I have eaten, each person I have known, each room in which I have slept. As ordinary as it all appears, there are times when it is beyond my imagination.

A meeting of two worlds

[4] **inconceivable** not understandable [5] **to hurl** to throw

Activities

Immigrants' experiences

1. Describe the different experiences of living an immigrant's life expressed in the two excerpts.
2. Analyse how the different attitudes can be related to basic concepts.

Between integration and detachment

3. Show why the author has chosen a panel discussion in the text *Confused Identity* to expand upon the topic of immigration.
4. Explain how the author explicitly and implicitly shows Gogol's detachment from his fellow Indians.

Immigration in the context of globalisation

5. Show how the young and the old generations in the text *The Achievement Beyond Imagination* represent different attitudes towards immigration.
6. How do you interpret the narrator's explanation of his immigrant experience, when he says that "there are times when it is beyond my imagination" (ll. 37f.)?
7. Discuss the statement that migration and immigration are the two most dramatic forms of globalisation.

Democracy and the Word of Allah

Orhan Pamuk

Globalisation has led to an exchange of ideas, among which the democratic self-determination of the individual, the division of church and state, the freedom of the press and equal rights for women count among the more prominent "export goods" of the West. These values often led and still lead to political, social and religious conflicts, to a "clash of civilisations" in countries trying to defend their history and their autonomy.
This fundamental conflict is illustrated in the novel *Snow*, which won Orhan Pamuk the Nobel Prize in 2006. It is about the journey of Ka, a Turkish poet living in exile in Frankfurt, Germany. Ka has gone back to Kars, a Turkish town on the border to Armenia, to find out what made young Muslim women wearing the veil commit suicide. He witnesses a military coup following the assassination of the director of the Institute of Education who had openly objected to religiously motivated suicides. The conversation between Ka and Blue, the representative of political Islam in Turkey, is one of his many encounters to grasp the fundamental difference between Eastern and Western thinking. An insurmountable obstacle?

Pay special attention ▼ to what Ka is going to publish in a paper.

For a long tense moment, the two stared at each other.
"Yesterday you told me that you had every intention of writing about the suicide girls in the Western press," said Blue.
Remembering his little lie, Ka felt embarrassed.
"Which Western newspaper did you have in mind?" Blue now asked.
"At which of the German papers do you have contacts?"
"The *Frankfurter Rundschau,*" said Ka.
"Who?"
"It's a liberal German newspaper."
"What's his name?"
"Hans Hansen," Ka said, and hugged[1] his coat.
"I have a statement for Hans Hansen. I intend to speak up against the coup," said Blue. "We don't have much time. I want you to start writing it down this instant."

Ka opened to the back page of his poetry notebook and began to take notes. Blue began by saying that at least eighty people had been killed so far (the actual death toll, including those shot at the theater, was seventeen); numerous schools and houses had been raided[2] and tanks had destroyed nine shanties[3] (the real figure was four); after claiming that some students had died under torture, he alluded to some street skirmishes[4] that Ka had not heard anyone else mention; passing rather quickly over the sufferings of the Kurds, he slightly exaggerated those visited on the Islamists; it was, he now said, to provide a pretext for this coup that the state had arranged for the mayor and the director of the Institute of

---

[1] **to hug** to hold tightly [2] **to raid** to attack [3] **shanty** primitive hut [4] **skirmish** short military engagement

Education to be assassinated. The reason for all this, he said, was to prevent the Islamists from winning the elections. The banning of all political parties and associations proved his point, he said.
As he went into more detail, Ka looked straight into Kadife's[5] eyes; she hung on Blue's every word. In the margins of these pages he would later tear out of his poetry notebook, he made a number of drawings and doodles that proved he was thinking about Ipek[6]: a slender neck, a head of hair, a child's house with childish smoke rising out of a child's chimney. ...
Many years before, Ka had explained to me that when a good poet is confronted with difficult facts that he knows to be true but also inimical[7] to poetry, he has no choice but to flee to the margins; it was, he said, this very retreat that allowed him to hear the hidden music that is the source of all art.
Ka appreciated some of Blue's pronouncements enough to record them in his notebook word for word.

> Contrary to what the West seems to think, it is not poverty that brings us so close to God; it's the fact that no one is more curious than we are to find out why we are here on earth and what will happen to us in the next world.

Instead of explaining the source of this curiosity and revealing mankind's purpose on earth, Blue's final words posed a challenge to the West:

> Will the West, which takes democracy, its great invention, more seriously than the word of God, come out against this coup that has brought an end to democracy in Kars? [He stopped here to make a grand gesture.] Or are we to conclude that democracy, freedom, and human rights don't matter, that all the West wants is for the rest of the world to imitate them like monkeys? Can the West endure any democracy achieved by enemies who in no way resemble them? I have something to say to all the other nations that the West has left behind: Brothers, you're not alone.

He paused for a moment. "Can you be sure that your friend at the *Frankfurter Rundschau* is going to print all this?"
"He takes offense when people discuss the West as if it's a single person with a single point of view," Ka said carefully.

◄ **Look at Ka's objections.**

"But that's how it is," Blue said, after another pause. "There is, after all, only one West and only one Western point of view. And we take the opposite point of view."
"The fact remains that they don't live that way in the West," said Ka. "It's not as it is here; they don't want everyone thinking alike. Everyone, even the most ordinary grocer, feels compelled to boast of having his own personal views. If we used the term *Western democrats* instead of *the West*, you'd have a better chance of pricking people's consciences[8]."
"Fine, do what you think best. Must we make more corrections to get this published?"
"Although this began as a news item, it's become more interesting, more like a proclamation," said Ka. "They might want to put your name to it ... and maybe even include a few biographical details –"

---

[5] **Khadife** the woman in love with Blue, Ipek's sister [6] **Ipek**, the woman in love with Ka
[7] **inimical** harmful [8] **to prick one's conscience** to stir your awareness of what is morally acceptable

"I've prepared those already," said Blue. "All they need say is that I'm one of the most prominent Islamists in Turkey and perhaps the entire Middle East."

"Hans Hansen is not going to print this as it stands."

"What?"

"If the social-democratic *Frankfurter Rundschau* were to print a statement from a single Turkish Islamist[9], it would seem as if they were taking sides," Ka said.

Observe Blue's ▶ interpretation of the West's reaction.

"I see. When something doesn't serve Mr. Hans Hansen's interests, he has a way of slithering away," said Blue. "What do we need to do to convince him?"

"Even if the German democrats come out against a military coup in Turkey – and it has to be a real coup, not a theatrical one – they'll still be very uneasy if the people they're defending are Islamists."

"Yes, these people are all terrified of us," said Blue.

Ka could not tell if he was boasting or merely feeling misunderstood. "Well," he said, "if you included the signatures of a liberal ex-Communist and a Kurdish nationalist, you'd have no trouble getting this announcement into the *Frankfurter Rundschau*."

---

[9] **Turkish Islamist** believer insisting on the supremacy of Islamic law over secular state law instituted by Kemal Ataturk

Activities

The conversation between Ka and Blue

1. Describe the situation and give a brief outline of the content of the conversation.
2. Relate it to what information you get about the author.

Linguistic and formal devices

3. Explain to what extent the opposition of the two characters is reflected in
   a) structure,
   b) argumentation and
   c) use of language.

A press comment and readers' reactions

4. Write Ka's press comment concentrating on obstacles to globalisation as apparent in this interview.
   Or:
   Write a letter to the editor explaining possible reader's responses to the advertisement on the right which appeared in the German press.

The newspaper. Those who read, understand.

A Migrant Looking for Work

T. Coraghessan Boyle

There is hardly a notion or an institution more diametrically opposed to the concept of globalisation than that of the frontier or the border. It may take different forms, its essential quality is that it divides one from the other, one nation from another, one hemisphere like that of the West from the East or the North from the South, one political or social system or a certain religion from the other, or simply the industrially and technologically advanced nations or regions from the disadvantaged ones. Very often it just comes down to the separation of the rich from the poor, from those who need workers and those who are looking for work, the basis of a more decent way of life and a better future for themselves and their families.
T. Coraghessan Boyle's novel *The Tortilla Curtain* introduces Cándido and his young wife, América (!), illegal immigrants in Southern California where Cándido hopes to find work and later a place to live and raise his family. The excerpt is about his frustrating work experience, which forms a stark contrast to the positive side of globalisation.

▼ Observe Cándido's work experience.

And then he got work five days in a row. Brush clearance. Hard hot dirty work, breathing dust and little pale flecks[1] of crushed weed[2] till you choked[3], and the sun beating at the back of your neck like a scourge[4] and the seeds of all those incorrigible[5] desert plants like needles, like fisherman's hooks stabbing through your clothes into your flesh every time you moved, and all you did was move. Three dollars and twenty-five cents an hour and he wasn't complaining. A *gabacho*[6] boss had pulled into the labor exchange lot[7] in a truck with high wooden sides, picked Cándido and another man and pantomimed what he wanted. They got in the back of his truck, five mornings in a row, and he took them to a canyon with eight new houses in it and they cleared brush from the hillside and raked it up and loaded it into the truck. Each afternoon he paid them in cash and each morning he was there again, seven a.m., regular as clockwork. On the fifth day, when work was finished, he didn't show them any money, but with gestures and a few gar-

An ambigous warning

[1] **fleck** small particle [2] **weed** any plant growing wild [3] **to choke** not to be able to get your breath [4] **scourge** like sth. which causes pain [5] **incorrigible** here: firmly rooted
[6] **gabacho** (*Mexican-Span.*) white man [7] **lot** parking area

bled Spanish phrases he let them know that he was short and would pay them when he came to pick them up in the morning. Cándido wondered about that, especially since they'd scraped the hillside bare[8], right down to the dirt, but then maybe there was another canyon and another hillside. There wasn't. At least not for Cándido. He never saw the man again.

All right. He'd been cheated before – it wasn't the first time. He would survive it. But then he didn't get work, not that day or the next or the day after that, and he came dragging back into camp at one each afternoon, dejected and heartsick with worry, and he let América fuss over him in her big maternity shorts while the worry trailed[9] off into boredom and the boredom into rage. But he controlled himself. América was innocent. She was everything to him. He had no one to rage at but himself and he raged internally till he had to get up and move, use his hands, do something, anything. [...]

Find out why Cándido ▼ was more lucky the next day.

The next morning he was up at first light, as usual, blowing into his coffee while América fried eggs, chilies and *tortillas* over a smokeless fire, and then he made his way up the hill to the labor exchange, feeling optimistic, lucky even, the wings of the little birds soaring in his veins. The limp was gone now – or almost gone – and though his face would never look quite the same again, at least the crust of scab[10] had fallen away, giving back some of the flesh beneath. He wasn't planning on entering any beauty contests anyway, but at least now the *patrones* in the trucks wouldn't automatically look past him to the next man. The sky swelled with light. He began to whistle through his teeth.

Out of habit he kept his head down as he walked along the side of the road, not wanting to risk making eye contact with any of the *gringos* or *gringas*[11] on their way to work in their unblemished[12] new Japanese cars. To them he was invisible, and that was the way he wanted to keep it, showing himself only in the lot at the labor exchange, where they could see what he was and what he had to offer. He barely glanced up at the tumult in the lot at the Chinese grocery – the sweet buns, coffee in styrofoam cups, frantic[13] cigarettes – and he didn't really lift his head until he felt the gravel of the labor exchange lot under his feet. He was wondering idly if he'd be first in line, thinking of the day ahead, whistling a radio tune he hadn't heard in years, when he looked up and it hit him: *there was nothing there*. No pillars, no roof, no *campesinos*[14] in khaki shirts and straw hats. Nothing. It was as if a hurricane wind had come up in the night, a tornado, and sucked the whole thing up into the sky. Cándido stood there, dumbstruck[15], and looked round him twice to get his bearings[16] . Was he dreaming? Was that it? [...]

"Looks closed," the man beside him put in.

"Yeah," the first man said, and his voice was lifeless, "looks like the *gabachos* don't want us here anymore." He dropped the stub of his cigarette in the street, shoved his hands in his pockets. "I don't give a shit," he said. "I'm going to stand right here till somebody hires me – it's a free country, isn't it?"

"Sure," Cándido said, and the way he was feeling he couldn't hold back the sarcasm, "– as long as you're a *gringo*. But us, we better look out."

---

[8] **bare** not covered [9] **to trail off** to become weaker [10] **scab** dried surface of healing skin [11] **gringo/gringa** (*Span.*) foreigner [12] **unblemished** immaculate, spotless [13] **frantic** like mad [14] **campesino** (*Span.*) worker on a farm [15] **dumbstruck** completely taken by surprise [16] **bearing** here: orientation

Activities

Hopes and reality

1. Describe Cándido's situation, his expectations and his experiences.
2. Give a brief description of the working conditions of the migrant workers.

The creation of authenticity

3. Analyse the point of view and explain what it contributes to the authenticity of the situation.
4. What do the references in Spanish and the dialogue reveal about the status of the migrants?

The fatal dilemma

5. Against the background of what you have read about globalisation, discuss Boyle's point of view. How would you explain the novelist's sceptical outlook?
6. Migrants usually know what to expect on the other side of the border. What makes them come nevertheless?
7. The text supplies an example of the migrants working on the land. Use the Internet to find out about migrants working in "sweatshops".

Transformation Through Tourism

Diana Darling

The latest information is available at a mouse-click and all sorts of TV programmes cover all aspects of the most exotic destinations: The world has been brought to our doorstep and has been reduced to a global village. But even though the virtual world is at our fingertips, we still want to see for ourselves, want to get the feeling of it. Now this long-cherished dream of mankind has come true.

The technological advancement in the field of logistics and transportation, an unsurpassed standard of living in the Western world with literally dollars to burn, a common interest in the hitherto unknown areas of the world and, above all, the democratisation of travelling have created a boom in worldwide travel. Among the most serious consequences of all this are the global environmental side-effects and the transformation of a so far unspoiled and authentic world.

South-east Asia and the Far East are just about ten hours away from home. Countries like Indonesia, formerly connected to Europe through the colonial powers of the Netherlands and Britain, have now become tourist magnets attracting millions of visitors every year. Tourism is a major source of income not only for the state but also for the average citizen and even for the remotest rural regions. This constant flow of tourists from the Western world has also led to a deeper understanding of a different cultural and religious heritage, which, however, some are ready to defend with force against the tide of "invaders". On the other hand, the reaction of the Western countries after the tsunami showed a globalised feature of solidarity and shows that tourism is not only about exploitation. Diana Darling, in a sort of modern fairy tale, has a critical and amused look at the latest development in globalisation, especially at how it works in concrete terms.

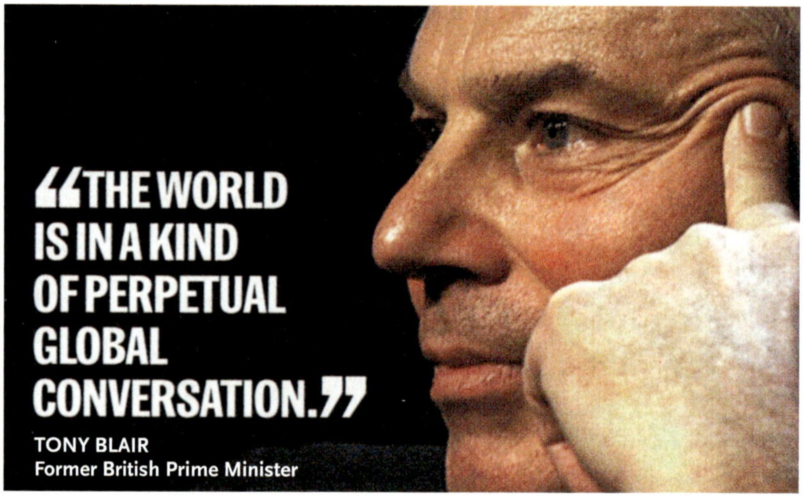

One day the young prince of Mameling summoned a dozen of the most influential villagers. He told them (after they'd all sipped glasses of coffee and lit up the free cigarettes) something like this:

"The future of Mameling is in tourism. Our foreign guests are powerful people in their own countries. They do us a great honor by showing so much interest in our culture. Do you know what culture is?"

There was a short silence.

"Culture is the way we do things. The tourists do things differently; they have a different culture – a very poor one, which is why they are so interested in ours. They have lots of money, yes, but they know nothing about the gods; they can't dance or play music (except for their own sort on radios); they don't understand rice, and many of them don't even eat rice."

This produced a roar of laughter from the men.

"So we have to make the tourists feel welcome and comfortable and provide them with the things they need. Now, what do tourists need? And what can we provide them with?"

A rhetorical pause, while the puzzled group sat waiting.

"They need to buy things. And after they buy things, they need a cold drink of beer. They need to eat and sleep – just as we do, but they need to eat in a tourist way and sleep in a tourist way. And they don't know how to go to the river."

Another roar of laughter.

Note the ambiguous ► role of the young prince.

"They need bathrooms, like the Chinese in Denpasar[1]. We'll talk about all this eating and sleeping and bathing in a minute. Now, what do the tourists want to buy? They will try to buy anything, everything. But we're poor people! [This was another rhetorical device; the prince was in fact very rich, and it was the villagers who were poor. No one dared to mention this, of course.] We must use our heads and our hands to make things for the tourists to buy. Some of us can paint – let's make paintings for the tourists. Some of us can carve – let's make sculpture for the tourists ... or jewelry, if we're good at that. Perhaps our children can dance. Let's have them dance

[1] **Denpasar** town in Indonesia, Bali

for the tourists! But let us protect our heirlooms[2]. Don't sell your krises[3]. Don't sell your silver offering bowls and the fine old carvings from your house temples. Let us protect our heritage, our *culture*!"

They let this pass, too. It was well known that the prince had made spectacular sales of palace treasures.

"Now. How do we make the tourists comfortable? We all have a bit of extra space in our compounds to build a guest house. How do we do this? First, we get a license, and then we build a nice little house and put in a new bed – it must be new, with a new mattress, pillow, and blanket – and on the porch we give them a chair to sit on. That's right, a chair, just like the one I'm sitting on, but it doesn't have to be as nice as this one – this is from the court in Yogyakarta[4] and is three hundred years old [actually it was Dutch, from Denpasar, circa 1912]. You can put a nice little bamboo chair on the porch for your tourist and a nice little bamboo table for his glass of tea."

One of the men asked the prince if he could explain about the bathroom.

"Very important. It has to be inside the little guest house. That's right, they want the bathroom indoors. And nobody in your family may use it when you have your tourist living there. And you must give your tourist his own private towel. Now here's how it works ..."

And so Mameling entered the age of "cultural tourism". Soon foreigners were seen everywhere, standing in people's way at the market, milling around in the temples, walking half-undressed and sweaty through the countryside, and forever holding black boxes in front of their faces. The foreigners were ugly, but they were very friendly and hilariously stupid, particularly with their money, of which they seemed to have unlimited amounts. All of this meant great changes for Mameling.

▼ Observe the image of the tourist and tourism.

◄ Look at the "blessings" of the age of "cultural tourism".

---

[2] **heirloom** what has been in your family for generations [3] **kris** short sword or dagger with a wavy blade [4] **Yogyakarta** city in Indonesia

Activities

Development of tourism

1. Sum up the stages of development of the tourist industry in the Indonesian villages.
2. Analyse the prince's ambiguous role in this process.

Point of view and irony

3. Study closely the role and the function of the author's choice of point of view as a device to influence the reader.
4. Look for examples of irony and explain what they reveal.

Your opinion

5. Write down the pros and cons of tourism.
6. What aspects of Third World tourism apply to tourism in general?
7. Some critics call this development another form of "economic or cultural imperialism". Write a comment.

Project work

8. Collect examples of advertisements from countries worldwide and show how they try to "sell" their country to tourists.

The Good Daughter, in a Brothel

Nicholas D. Kristof

Travelling to distant and exotic parts of the world is no longer a privilege of the few who can afford it, but is part of worldwide mass tourism. Long before environmentalists and climatologists raised objections, human rights organisations and especially feminist activists protested against what they called sex tourism. Cheap air fares and low rates for accommodation generally attractive for all kinds of tourists from the backpacker to the nature lover and the families, also encouraged men to fly to South-East Asia to seek cheap sexual adventures and exploit the misery of the female population, very often teenage girls. The greater the poverty and despair of the population, the harsher and tragic the effects of a globalisation gone wrong.

Note the abvious ▼ change of a cliché.

One of the oldest social dichotomies[1] is the one dividing good girls from bad, the Madonna from the whore[2]. But in poor countries where sex trafficking and globalization have fostered[3] new forms of slavery, it is the saintly ones – those who risk leaving their villages to help their families – who often end up as whores.

Yan Kosal is a 26-year-old woman here in northwestern Cambodia who was devoted to her aging parents and concerned with providing for them. Her mother is blind, her father is frail, and they depend on her – the only surviving child – for food.

Kosal earned only $30 a month as a peddler[4], barely enough to scrape by. So when a woman acquaintance told her that she could earn $90 a month selling snacks in Thailand, Kosal leapt at the opportunity.

"I thought I should do this to feed my parents," Kosal said, particularly because her acquaintance offered to escort her to Bangkok. Kosal borrowed $15 to pay her travel expenses, and they set out in September. But once they were in Thailand, where Kosal couldn't speak the language, the trafficker sold her to a brothel.

"First, I cried," Kosal said. But the brothel manager beat Kosal until she capitulated. "If the men wanted to go to the room," Kosal said numbly[5], "the girl had to go." The women were paid nothing, except for tips – but the sad ones who wept and were uncooperative didn't get tips.

Look at the ▼ conclusions and generalisations.

It's difficult to gauge[6] how common such forced prostitution is. But it appears that in much of Asia the entry into prostitution is overwhelmingly unwilling (and in any case, the girls are typically too young to give consent). Then once they have been stigmatized and have lost hope of returning to their families and villages – and in some cases become addicted to drugs – they often accept their lot and continue without coercion[7].

As for Kosal, she did manage to escape. Last month she and another young woman fled their brothel in the middle of the night and set off to walk back to Cambodia.

---

brothel place where men pay prostitutes to have sex [1] **dichotomy** classification into two opposite parts [2] **whore** prostitute [3] **to foster** to develop [4] **peddler** person selling illegal drugz [5] **numb** without feeling [6] **to gauge** ['geidz] to measure [7] **coercion** force

Cambodian girl hoping for a better future

Activities

Prostitution in South East Asia

1. As can be seen in newspaper articles, give subtitles to the key paragraphs.
2. Then explain the conditions particular to this region that help to promote prostitution in South East Asia.

Clichés reversed

3. Explain the overall argumentative structure of the article.
4. Point out the use of language which characterises this article.

A new form of slavery

5. The author compares child prostitution to slavery. State to what extent this is justified.
6. Very often low prices in the Western hemisphere are the result of exploitation (e.g. child labour) of the Third World. Comment on the dilemma of the victims.
7. Suggest ways to prevent this form of exploitation.

Acknowledgements

Illustrations

p. 4: Matthias Berghahn/Verlagsarchiv Schöningh; p. 5: Reinhild Kassing/ Verlagsarchiv Schöningh; p. 6 top left: dpa-Fotoreport, Ingo Wagner; p. 6 bottom left: Toyota; p. 6 center, right: Günter Schlottmann/Verlagsarchiv Schöningh; p. 7: © 2007 The Coca-Cola Company; p. 11: Susanne Baumann/Verlagsarchiv Schöningh; p. 12: Dyson; p. 13 left: taken from: auto, motor und sport Spezial 2006; p. 13 right (3 photos): © 2006 TVR Cars Distribution Ltd.; p. 15: Misereor; p. 17 top, 20, 22, 38, 40, 59: © picture-alliance/dpa; p. 17 bottom: eins Entwicklungspolitik; p. 18: © Lineair/Das Fotoarchiv; p. 19: © REUTERS/Thomas Mukoya; p. 23: Simon Kneebone; p. 24: Copyright Martin Rowson 1998; p. 25: Pumpkin House; p. 26: © Arco/ U. Walz; p. 27: taken from The Economist, October 9, 2004, p. 63; p. 29: Austin; p. 32: © argum/Thomas Einberger; p. 34: Image courtesy of Pedro Sanchez, Earth Institute at Columbia University; p. 35: action press/REX FEATURES LTD.; p. 36: Miel, CWS/Cartoonarts International; p. 37: Photograph by Charles Ommanney; p. 39: Andrzej Krauze; p. 42: Wolfgang Horsch; p. 43: Oguz Gurel; p. 45: Copyrighted by the White House Historical Association, photograph by the National Geographic Society; p. 46: © dpa/ Rauchwetter; p. 48: taken from The Economist, December 16, 2006, p. 7; p. 50: taken from Time, February 26, 2007; p. 52: Solange Brand; p. 55: © 20th Century Fox/Cinetext; p. 56: John Giles – AP; p. 58: Bundesverband Deutscher Zeitungsverleger (Berlin)/ZMG Zeitungs Marketing Gesellschaft (Frankfurt) und Ogilvy&Mather (Frankfurt); p. 62: Joel Saget – AFP/Getty Images; p. 65: © picture-alliance/ZB; others: Verlagsarchiv Schöningh

Texts

Martin Wolf: "What Drives Globalisation?" from "Will Globalisation Survive?" in *Financial Times*, April 5, 2005

"Open Markets – Economic Liberalisation" from "Open Markets Matter: The Benefits of Trade and Investment Liberalisation" in *OECD Observer*, October 1999, www.oecd.org/dataoecd/18/51/1948792.pdf [25.05.07] and M. Suppermaniam: "Globalisation and Economic Liberalisation – Implications on the Public Service" in *Buletin JPA Online*, www.jpa.gov.my/buletinjpa/bil2/globalisation_and_economic_liber.htm [05.03.2007]

"Moving the Manufacture of Cleaners to Malaysia" from *The Guardian*, December 10, 2004

Mark Milner: "TVR to Move its Production Abroad" from "TVR to Axe 250 Jobs and Shift Sports Car Production Abroad" in *The Guardian*, October 19, 2006

Jeremy Rifkin: "Return of a Conundrum" from *The Guardian*, March 2, 2004

Henry Ekwuruke: "Globalisation and the Developing World" from *AfricaFront – International News Network*, www.africafront.com/news/136/globalization_and_the_developing_world.html [02.02.07]

"Kenya: Focus on Working Conditions in EPZ Companies" from *IRIN News*, March 9, 2004, www.irinnews.org/report.aspx?reportid=48975 [25.05.07] Copyright © IRIN 2007

James Howard Kunstler: "Globalisation is an Anomaly and its Time is Running Out" from *The Guardian*, August 4, 2005

Michael Meacher: "End of the World Nigh – It's Offcial" from *The Guardian*, February 14, 2003

Craig Donnellan: "The Kyoto Protocol – The Background" from *The Global Debate*, ed. by Craig Donnellan, Cambridge, Independence, 2001, p. 16

Mark Lynas: "Take Personal Action to Reduce Emissions" from *High Tide. News from a Warming World* by Mark Lynas, London, Flamingo, 2004, pp. 291 – 294

Jeffrey D. Sachs: "Living in Poverty – Dying of AIDS" from *The End of Poverty. How We Can Make It Happen in Our Lifetime* by Jeffrey D. Sachs, London, Penguin, 2005, pp. 5 – 10

"Confronting Poverty", Editorial from *Süddeutsche Zeitung/The New York Times*, May 17, 2003, p. 2

Niall Ferguson: "The Logic of Terror" from *Colossus. The Price of America's Empire* by Niall Ferguson, New York, Penguin, 2004, pp. 119 – 121

Farreed Zakaria: "The Best Ways to Beat Terror" from *Newsweek*, April 12, 2004, p. 17

George W. Bush: "Remarks at the United Nations General Assembly" from www.whitehouse.gov/news/releases/2002/09/20020912-1.html [25.5.07]

"New World Order – Remaking the United Nations" from *The Guardian*, March 11, 2003

Jim Garrison: "The Future Role of America" from *America as Empire. Global Leader or Rogue Power?* by Jim Garrison, San Francisco, Berret-Koehler Publishers, 2004, pp. 199 – 202

Kofi Annan: "The Farewell Address" from www.newsobserver.com/559/v-print/story/520366.html [12.12.2006], © Copyright 2007, The News Observer Publishing Company

Dai Sijie: "Western Literature as Eye-Opener" from *Balzac and the Little Chinese Seamstress* by Dai Sijie, London, Vintage, 2001, pp. 101 – 103

Jhumpa Lahiri: "Confused Identity". Excerpt from THE NAMESAKE: A Novel by Jhumpa Lahiri. Copyright © 2003 by Jhumpa Lahiri. Reprinted by permission of Houghton Mifflin Company. All rights reserved.

Jhumpa Lahiri: "The Achievement Beyond Imagination". Excerpt from "The Third and Final Continent", from INTERPRETER OF MALADIES by Jhumpa Lahiri. Copyright © 1999 by Jhumpa Lahiri. Reprinted by permission of Houghton Mifflin Company. All rights reserved.

Orhan Pamuk: "Democracy and the Word of Allah" from *Snow* by Orhan Pamuk, London, Faber & Faber, 2005, pp. 227 – 229

T. Coraghessan Boyle: "A Migrant Looking for Work" from *The Tortilla Curtain* by T. Coraghessan Boyle, London, Bloomsbury, 1996, pp. 195–198

Diana Darling: "Transformation Through Tourism" from "The Painted Alphabet" by Diana Darling, in *Planet Earth. Egotists and Ecosystems*, ed. by Roger Rosen and Patra McSharry, New York, The Rosen Publishing Group, 1991, pp. 4–6

Nicholas D. Kristof: "The Good Daughter, in a Brothel" from *The New York Times*, January 2, 2007